GOURMET MEALS in Crappy Little Kitchens

Jennifer Schaertl

Health Communications, Inc.
Deerfield Beach, Florida

www.hcibooks.com

Library of Congress Cataloging-in-Publication Data

Schaertl, Jennifer.
    Gourmet meals in crappy little kitchens / Jennifer Schaertl.
        p. cm.
    Includes index.
    ISBN-13: 978-0-7573-1365-3
    ISBN-10: 0-7573-1365-5
    1. Cookery.   I. Title.
TX714.S35 2010
641.5—dc22

                                                                                    2010002238

HCI, its logos, and marks are trademarks of Health Communications, Inc.

Publisher: Health Communications, Inc.
        3201 S.W. 15th Street
        Deerfield Beach, FL 33442-8190

Cover food photo ©Inmagine; author photo ©Jay Shirtz, jayshirtz.com
Cover design by Larissa Hise Henoch
Interior design and formatting by Lawna Patterson Oldfield

Contents

The Art of Cooking in Your Crappy Little Kitchen

I know what you're thinking . . . *Gourmet Meals in Crappy Little Kitchens,* isn't that an oxymoron? You actually couldn't be further from the truth! Chef Francois Vatel, not only invented Chantilly cream (vanilla sweetened whipped cream) without the aid of a motorized mixer, but he also created ice sculptures for his table displays in 1671 with ice he foraged from the great outdoors. While preparing dinner for King Louis XIV, Vatel learned that the fish for the meal would not arrive on time. So distraught with embarrassment, he ran himself through with his own sword. While I'm sure your Crappy Little Kitchen has introduced many cooking conundrums and you can identify with Vatel's pain, I can assure you there is no need for desperate measures when it comes to making the most of your Crappy Little Kitchen. With my help, your Crappy Little Kitchen will become the centerpiece for delicious gourmet meals and a place you will love to call home.

Crappy Little Kitchens rock, and if you give your Crappy Little Kitchen (CLK for short) half a chance, you'll be in complete agreement. When I made lobster for my friends in what was essentially a tiny bedroom on the second floor of a Brooklyn brownstone, with a teeny sink, tiny stove, and hotel-room-size refrigerator (I tower over it at 5'7") all just shoved up against the wall, I found the experience much more inspiring!

Cooking in a CLK builds character and personality— two attributes of downright delicious gourmet meals. And I will teach you everything you need to know so you will love your CLK and the food that comes out of it.

The first restaurant where I became the sous chef wasn't much bigger than a closet. The dishwashing machine was crammed so close to the stove that I stood with my back touching the dishwasher as he worked by my side. While training a new line cook, I asked her to please juice a small bag of lemons for a fresh vinaigrette. When she asked me where my juicer was, I responded by

1

lifting my right hand with a look on my face that said, "You're looking at it!"

Whatever your kitchen situation—whether you have a minuscule space, ancient appliances, or a dismal appearance (or all three!)—you can still work wonders and create gourmet meals. The reason I am so confident about this fact is that growing up I witnessed my father perform what others might think is a mealtime miracle—he baked a delicious pineapple upside-down cake using a campfire. So, if Dad can do cozy comfort food in the great outdoors, there is no stopping what creations await in Crappy Little Kitchens!

Using a Dutch oven that's been in my father's family for generations, he layers brown sugar, sliced pineapple, and a little pineapple juice to make the caramel. He pours a very simple vanilla sponge cake recipe over the top and covers it with the cast iron lid. Using red hot coals he pulls from the fire we've been visiting around all evening, my father places his Dutch oven over them. He scoops more coals onto the top, and the family conjures an image of the brown sugar and juice beginning to bubble and pop into caramel around the softening pineapple, whose steam has begun to make the cake batter rise ever so evenly. In short order, my father pulls the cake from the fire to unveil it, and we are quiet for the first time since—well since the last time my dad made the cake! Look for Dad's Miraculous Campfire Cake recipe CLK style in the Desserts to Die For section of this book.

Just because you cook in a CLK does not justify a crappy meal!

What Is Gourmet?

I created this book to bring gourmet cooking into your home and your CLK. Gourmet meals don't need to be intimidating or overly complicated, although the word gourmet tends to strike fear in some and inspire awe in others. It can be a proper noun describing a person with discriminating tastes and a well-defined palate for fine food and drink. It can also be an adjective to describe a type of restaurant, menu, or cook. The definition I prefer, which applies to *Gourmet Meals in Crappy Little Kitchens*, is food perfectly prepared from the finest ingredients and artfully presented with love and care.

What I like to emphasize (especially when people tell me how they dread cooking for me because they shudder to think what I will think) is that the meaning of gourmet is subjective. How do you take an everyday dish like macaroni and cheese and heighten it to the level of gourmet? Truffles, an interesting blend of fine cheeses, and homemade pasta is one way. Or you can follow a basic macaroni and cheese recipe, and prepare it perfectly. Nicely seasoned, al dente, store-bought noodles and a well-executed cheddar cheese sauce can make a gourmet meal. Both dishes constitute a gourmet creation because they both comprise a blend of flavors and textures, artful presentations, and the freshest foods possible. You don't need every ingredient, just like you don't need every kitchen tool made to man to create a gourmet meal. What is essential are the best ingredients available to you, prepared with an expertise that comes with practice and respect for food preparation. A little experimentation thrown in doesn't hurt, either! Whether you make the most complicated salmon soufflé or a delicious smoothie, all you need is practice,

> My Crappy Little Kitchen experiences molded me into a better chef and a better person than I was before, and your CLK experiences can do the same for you.

practice, practice! It's *way* more fun to practice in a Crappy Little Kitchen where you only need the basic tools of the trade and no complicated contraptions to distract you!

A Journey Through My Crappy Little Kitchens

Besides witnessing resourceful cooking firsthand from my dad, I learned the art of cooking in a Crappy Little Kitchen from, well, cooking in Crappy Little Kitchens. My first Crappy Little Kitchen was in a one-room efficiency apartment where I could flip an egg on the stove while sitting in my living room. In my next apartment, my CLK was so small I had to use my cutting board on my washing machine. Although my washing machine was inoperable (go figure!), it served a useful purpose by acting as additional counter space.

My next apartment move landed me in my very favorite CLK in Sunset Park, Brooklyn, where I'm convinced "Jennifer the Chef" was born. I've had several Crappy Little Kitchens since and live with one right now. I'm still larger than my refrigerator and my kitchen floor slopes terribly causing my ancient stove to sway back and forth. I have terrible storage and no dishwasher, well, unless you count me.

Gourmet Meals in Crappy Little Kitchens offers you practical hints and tips to make the most of your CLK space and shows you exactly how to re-create the delicious gourmet meals that I've served as a chef in several five-star restaurants over the last eight years. I created and perfected all of the gourmet meals that make up this book in my own CLK, and I'll share my chef secrets with you. But what you will gain the most from me is my CLK expertise. You'll learn kitchen shortcuts, surprising factoids, space saving ideas, and frugal hints, and I'll introduce you to new and delicious foods. I'll expand your cooking repertoire with suggestions for unusual gourmet ingredients, but I'll always offer you simple alternatives without sacrificing taste. You'll discover a myriad of options for various methods of preparation and presentation. I'll also offer easy ideas for pairing recipes and ingredients for even greater variety by combining recipes included in this book. For example, serve the Fried Green Tomatoes with the Chipotle Aioli, and the Snake-Charmin' Moroccan Lamb Chops with the Kick Your Caboose Saffron Couscous. You can use your Crappy Little Kitchen to create kitchen magic. Don't fall prey to the misconception your crappy kitchen space limits your possibilities or confines your pallet. The opposite is true. My restaurant-proven experience shows fine food and cramped kitchen quarters are not mutually exclusive. So, let's take the stuffy out of gourmet. It's time to enjoy that beef tartar AND your mother's meatloaf, just perhaps not in the same sitting!

TOP FIVE REASONS
WHY CLKS ROCK MORE THAN GLITZY
GOURMET KITCHENS

1. CLKs take less time to clean.
2. Everything you need is within arm's reach and never gets lost.
3. Stainless steel leaves fingerprints.
4. Making physical contact with your partner, roommate, or friend is easy (and unavoidable) in your CLK.
5. You only have what you need and only need what you have.

Top-of-the line contemporary kitchens with all the luxurious amenities and newfangled shiny appliances do not make a good cook. The only real necessity for turning out gourmet meals is you! With my help, you will transform yourself into a fabulous cook and learn how your CLK provides the perfect landscape to elevate your cooking from pedestrian to perfection. Now there are first-class kitchens that are small in stature, and there are enormous kitchens with a stove, sink, and fridge shoved up against the wall. The important thing to remember is that your little kitchen, as crappy as it may be, is far superior to everyone else's. Wanna know why?

- Your kitchen is the "every kitchen." It's approachable, it's homey, it's where everyone gathers when you throw a party.
- Most people with super nice kitchens don't cook in them, because they don't want to mess up their gorgeous "show" kitchens. I will teach you how to be "hands on" in your CLK, and you'll barely make a mess when you cook.
- Making a beautiful meal in a grand kitchen looks easy and is always expected, but your guests will experience awe and wonder when you present them with eye-watering and delicious Braised Lamb Shank Shepherd's Pie straight from your crappy little stove.
- You may have the Crappiest Little Kitchen in your group of friends, but with my simple advice you'll be the best cook of the bunch.
- Fashions change, economies crash, people come and go, but you're Crappy Little Kitchen has survived the test of time. With its original subway tile, wobbly stove, and non-defrosting refrigerator that didn't start out "eggshell," your CLK will provide pleasure and gourmet meals for generations to come.

Where most people go awry in their CLK is in buying space-wasting gadgets. I'm here to tell you: never bother with a tool that only has one function! The kitchen gear I recommend not only does an excellent job at the function for which it is intended, it also can perform additional tasks making each item an invaluable tool for the gourmet cook confined to a small space. Invest in these CLK-friendly must-haves that will give you the most bang for your buck:

Pots and pans

You only need a few utilitarian pots and pans to do the job in your CLK. Make sure these are durable, heavy bottom pots preferably with matching lids (but foil makes a perfect crappy little lid). I prefer stainless steal (strong, resists rust, inexpensive, around $40, and usually dishwasher safe) with a copper or aluminum coil buried in the base for even heating. You don't need to buy the most expensive, but make sure they are able to go in the oven without warping the handles (it will say "oven safe" somewhere on the packaging, but if the entire thing is stainless steal you'll know it's oven safe).

12-quart stockpot with strainer and steamer basket

You can boil a box of spaghetti or steam large lobsters in this monster pot. You only need one large stockpot for all size jobs. Because it comes with its own steamer and strainer basket, which nestle inside for easy storage, you can also use this same pot for steaming vegetables as well as to strain the pasta or lobsters without the need for a separate colander. Use this pot to make any of the soup or sauce recipes found in this cookbook. You can prepare small or large quantities in this same pot.

12-inch stainless steel sauté pan

This generous sauté pan will work for jobs both large and small. You can fry two pieces of bacon, or make a monster party-size portion of paella in this magical pan. I use this pan more than any other pan in my kitchen, because I sauté, caramelize, or sweat onions and garlic, which is how I begin most of the meals in my kitchen.

8-inch nonstick sauté pan

Most chefs swear by stainless steel and refuse to use anything else. It's true that proteins like chicken or beef won't brown as well in a nonstick pan (mainly because you really shouldn't get nonstick pans that hot). If you don't scratch its surface or overheat it, nonstick is a spectacular invention. Eggs over easy are heaven on buttered toast, and fish get a crispy crust before sliding out of the pan with the greatest of ease.

1-quart stainless steel saucepot

This pot is the perfect size when making delicate sauces or reheating small amounts of soup. A larger surface area will retain heat better, and therefore cook much faster. When working butter into a sauce or reheating a velvety cream soup, this is the opposite of what you want. You need slow and low heat to prevent overheating or breaking your sauce or soup. It doesn't require much space and takes the place of a meat mallet when pounding out cutlets!

Dutch oven

A Dutch oven is a large pot or kettle with a tight fitting lid. You can choose from cast iron, ceramic, or even stainless steel, but what you need is something slightly smaller than a roasting pan. It should have a heavy bottom to go on the stovetop for baked beans, but also go in the oven for braised rabbit or pot roast. Now if you have a small roasting pan or braising pan, don't throw it away and buy a Dutch oven. This is a great example of using what you have. Make the Lamb Shank Sheppard's Pie in your braising pan and use a piece of foil as your lid.

Pot rack

This is very easy to make with a wire rack from an old barbeque grill, four strong ceiling hooks, four chains of equal length, and some "S" hooks. The look will add a bit of shabby chic to your Crappy Little Kitchen. The grill rack itself becomes the body of the pot rack. First, you must anchor the hooks into the ceiling. Just explain the project to the hardware store employee, and they'll steer you in the right direction for the items that you need. Once you've properly installed the hooks into the ceiling, hang the chains from the hooks, then hang the four "S" hooks from the bottom of each chain, and attach the grill rack. Hang the rest of the "S" hooks from the grill rack, arranging them equal distances apart. Start looking for stuff to hang from those hooks!

If you're not a do-it-yourselfer, you can also find reasonably priced pot racks in any store that boasts a kitchen section. With this nifty gadget, you can suspend pots and pans right above your head for easy reach, but most important, your lack of storage becomes a non-issue. Make the best use of your limited space by hanging all sorts of things from the ceiling, walls, or counters. Buy inexpensive under-the-counter wineglass holders and hanging wire baskets for your fruits and vegetables.

Utensils

You no longer need a meat mallet, since whacking the meat with your saucepan will serve that purpose, but having a few double-duty utensils can eliminate all sorts of unnecessary space-wasting gadgets. Keep all your thin handled utensils (spatula, spider, etc.) together in a decorative jar next to your stovetop for easy access, and you won't have to use up your limited drawer space.

Heat-resistant spatula

Usually made of silicone, a heat resistant spatula won't scratch your pans, melt, or catch fire. It takes the place of the wooden spoon and the metal spatula. A heat-resistant spatula flips eggs and burgers beautifully, and it will scrape every last drop from mixing bowls.

Whisk

One 12- to 16-inch, thin wire whisk is the only whisk you'll ever need. Whipping cream, working butter into a sauce, creaming eggs and sugar, sifting dry ingredients, and even whipping up mashed potatoes are all utilities of the whisk, so I do recommend owning one.

Tongs

In a professional kitchen, this is the most used utensil. You can turn meat, stir, move pots with hot handles around the stovetop, pick out food from poaching liquid, and you can even juice a lime with it. It's a great serving utensil for salad or asparagus, too! A nice lightweight aluminum pair of tongs is a great piece of equipment, and if there's no room left on the pot rack, you can hang it from a nail on the wall.

Spider

No, not an arachnid, but a nifty Asian-style utensil that looks like a shallow wire basket with a long handle and is great for lifting vegetables and pasta out of boiling water in fairly large batches. It keeps you from having to pull out broccoli one by one from blanching liquid or pouring out all your boiling water into a colander and starting over. If you need to strain the fat from a few pieces of meat or gently lift poached eggs, this is the tool to use.

Pastry brush

These guys are incredibly cheap, and I haven't found an acceptable substitute for brushing on butter, egg wash, and sauces. I can't think of a better way to apply glaze to a duck breast. You can also use it to spread herbs and spices, pesto, or condiments like whole grain mustard over your culinary creations. It's a great tool for spreading oil on your sheet tray, too.

Vegetable peeler

A vegetable peeler is great for peeling cucumbers, apples, and potatoes. It's also an excellent tool for shaving hard cheeses and slicing carrots into ribbons for a colorful salad display.

Knives

You only need three basic knives to perform every slicing and dicing task you can imagine as a gourmet chef. This discovery liberated me because knives can be one of the most costly items in your kitchen. Everything else the knife guy tries to sell you is either a glorified steak knife that belongs in the silverware drawer, or unnecessary equipment that will be perfectly happy taking up needed space in someone else's kitchen.

I keep my knives on a magnetic strip on the wall where I can easily grab them. This storage method is not only more hygienic than the old school butcher's block (knives may drip dry naturally rather than sit in a puddle inside the storage block) but also, a huge space saver. Imagine the great big chunk of counter space you'll save by not having that ugly block of wood on the counter. This way, the knives don't take up space, and you don't have to worry about getting grazed by a sharp blade or point as you would if you stored them in a drawer with other utensils. Look for the magnetic strip in a kitchen goods store. It's a snap to install and is a handy item you'll use every day.

6- to 8-inch chef's knife

This is the perfect utility knife, with a distinctive shape made famous by movie serial killers like Michael Meyers. Besides cutting, chopping, and slicing, you can use it to crush and peel garlic, carve meat, and even fillet a fish. When choosing a knife, hold it in your hand to see if it feels comfortable. If you have very small hands, a Santoku-style chef's knife will be perfect, because it has a shorter blade and a slightly curved and smaller handle. Always go with a stainless steel knife because it won't rust, and it holds a sharp edge very well, is relatively inexpensive and easy to sharpen if it does go dull. I use a very inexpensive handheld knife sharpener that has guards to prevent accidents, but if you don't own a knife sharpener it's not a necessity, since most places that sell knives can either sharpen them for you or refer you to someone who can. For cooking at home, I do not buy expensive knives. Shop for a comfortable, stainless steal knife priced around $40–$50, and you'll be pleased with your purchase.

Bread knife

Because it has a serrated edge, a bread knife can cut up a whole rib eye or carve a turkey, not to mention slice bread. Plus you'll need this tool for slicing cake layers whenever you can't find the dental floss (more on that later).

Paring knife

A paring knife, with its compact blade, is perfect for cutting small vegetables like radishes or for deveining shrimp.

Cutting board

For years, wood cutting boards received a bad rap because they were believed to harbor bacteria. As the proud owner of an heirloom wooden cutting board, I reserved its use for cutting vegetables, while using a plastic one for meat. New research refutes the old notion that wood is bad, and now scientists claim that wood, especially bamboo, actually has antibacterial properties. Cleaning a wooden cutting board is a breeze, just wipe it down with a soapy rag and give it a quick rinse with cool water. Very Crappy Little Cleanup friendly! Buy one good-size bamboo cutting board, and base that on how much counter space you have to lay it out on when in use. Mine is one by two feet, but if you don't have enough counter space for something that big, you can set it over two burners of your stove to chop and have very easy access to the pot next to you. If you have too many burners working, just place the board on a towel draped over your sink (the towel is to keep the board from slipping while you chop).

Bowls

I recommend buying one nestling set of three or four stainless steel mixing bowls. The very largest is for whipping cream, tossing vegetables in marinade, dressing a salad, or mixing a cake. The smallest is for stirring together the cornstarch and water for thickening your soup or whisking a couple of eggs for a small frittata. I like to have two in-between sizes, because I use them frequently and often need them both at the same time.

Glass bowls can go in the microwave and work well as double boilers but can also break and send glass shards all over your CLK. Ceramic bowls chip and break easily, are very heavy, and take up more room because of their thickness. Plastic can go in the microwave but can't go on or in the stove, and looks cheap and can stain. However, stainless steel is best because it won't break, can be used on the stove, and it takes up the least room when stacked together. A stainless steel bowl gets a good chill in the freezer, which makes it perfect for whipping cream, and if you don't beat them up too badly, they look very nice as serving bowls. Check out the next section to see what you need for melting chocolate in the microwave.

Measuring cups

One four-cup measuring cup set will take care of all your wet ingredient measuring needs. Make sure to buy a non-breakable, heat resistant one. Because of its high tolerance to heat, this measuring cup can go in the microwave for melting butter or chocolate, and you don't need to worry about glass chipping into any of your recipes. The packaging will let you know if it is resistant to heat and chipping. In addition, you'll need a set of multisize, fitted, round measuring cups (the material of these isn't that important), which are usually connected on a ring. You can level off dry ingredients and use these to portion out crab cakes or cookie dough. If they're on a ring, you can hang them from your pot rack or a nail in the wall.

Measuring spoons

They all hang out together on a ring and work out well for precise measurements of baking powder, spices, etc. Make sure to purchase metal ones because you can use them in place of a melon baller, and to hollow out tomatoes for stuffing. The plastic ones will probably snap under the pressure of either of these jobs.

Box cheese grater

It will tackle any grating or microplaning need you have and can hang from your pot rack. Each of the four sides has different size holes for making hash browns, grating ginger, or shaving truffles. It's also a useful tool for shredding cabbage or onions.

Fine strainer

Sometimes you need to strain a sauce to remove stems, seeds, or shells that might escape through the holes of a stockpot strainer. A fine strainer only costs a couple bucks and doesn't take up much room; in fact mine hangs from my pot rack. It also works well for sifting flour and dusting desserts with cocoa or powdered sugar.

Thermometer

You'll need one digital-read multipurpose food thermometer. It fool proofs the difference between medium rare and medium, prevents sugar from getting cooked past the soft ball stage, and perfectly regulates your frying oil in the saucepan, so you don't have to buy a fryer! The same one can work for meat or candy!

Sheet tray

Most home cooks are more familiar with the term cookie sheet, but it truly can do so much more than that. You can use it to toast nuts, or as a lid on a pot of water. You need one for roasting vegetables, and don't forget the cookies!

Cake pans

No one loves cakes more than I do, but I find I don't make them that often. For the recipes in this book, you'll only need a 6-inch and 8-inch springform pan. For all other cakes baked in my CLK, I purchase disposable pans. Grocery stores carry a variety of shapes and sizes so you don't need to store regular pans that you only use twice a year. If you find yourself making a lot of cakes, go ahead and buy the pan you need.

Blender

Luckily blenders come in various shapes and sizes, so you should be able to find one that will fit some nook or cranny in your house. A six-cup blender with three AMPS and two speeds is perfect for my home needs. Remember you don't need to store it in your kitchen if there's no room. Keep the box it came in, and when you're not using it, leave it in the hall or bedroom closet. A food processor is certainly helpful, but not necessary if you don't have the room.

Hang It!

Ceiling pot rack

Magnetic strip for Knives

Under-the-counter wineglass holder

Space-Saving Tools

12-quart stock pot with strainer and steamer basket

Spider utensil

French press

Hanging wire baskets

Lazy Susan

Rolling shelves in Kitchen cabinet

CLK Sab⊘teurs

Torch

You can buy the tiny one for too much money at your local kitchen gadget store, or you can go to the hardware store and buy a serious torch. A propane torch will caramelize a brulee in 30 seconds as opposed to that tiny butane one sold in a kitchen store that will take 5 minutes. It will come with a small propane canister that is very cheap to replace when it runs out, but chances are, it will last for years. I use mine for everything from caramelizing sugar on desserts to searing large pieces of meat.

CLK Saboteurs

Your kitchen is probably cluttered with a ridiculous number of unnecessary items that you've accumulated over time and stashed in every nook and cranny of your cramped space. How often have you used the ice cream maker from Auntie Ann or the trifle bowl from your wedding? Go through your kitchen cabinets and drawers and pull out every piece of useless equipment, unnecessary bowls, pans, and gadgets, and box them up. You only need the important tools I've recommended above, but if this causes a great concern for you, wait a year. If you haven't gone into the box because you needed something in one year, the whole box goes to charity. Someone needs that crap more than you!

In particular, you should unload the space-wasting, extraneous items, aka CLK Saboteurs that follow:

Colander

Because our stockpot comes with a built in strainer and a steamer basket, you have two colanders right there. One big, and one small.

Roasting pan

It's just too big! If you plan to roast a turkey or something huge, just buy a disposable pan for the occasion. Don't store that monstrosity of a roasting pan for the blue moon occasion when you cook an entire rib eye. A Dutch oven or braising pan can go in the stove or on the stove and will hold enough food to feed a small army. Give grandma her roasting pan back. You don't need it.

Meat mallet

This is my favorite example of CLK ingenuity! Don't buy or store a meat mallet. Pound out that chicken cutlet, crush those nuts with a heavy bottom saucepot, and tenderize that steak with a fork. Really.

Metal or wooden spoons and metal spatulas

One heat resistant spatula can take care of all your stirring and flipping needs. It comes clean much easier than a wooden spoon, and mine has a hole in the handle making it perfect to hang from the pot rack.

Sifter

My mom always used one of those old school flour sifters that looks like a tin can with a handle attached. This thing is the epitome of the one trick pony. In my CLK, I can't live without a whisk or a strainer and both can take the place of a sifter. A sifter, however, can't whip egg whites or strain out raspberry seeds (at least not very efficiently).

Melon baller

I'm kind of offended by balls of melon anyway. Think of all the melon that probably got thrown away, unless you were clever enough to put the scraps in a smoothie or fancy margarita! The Greek-Godlike Stuffed Tomatoes do need to be hollowed out, however, and a metal measuring spoon or even a dinner spoon will make short order of this.

Mandolin and microplanes

Now in my restaurants, I really can't live without a mandolin. We just slice and julienne in too much volume to use a box grater. In my home however, I only use my box cheese grater, which comes with three grating sides—fine, medium, and coarse, and one slicing side for slicing—for all my grating and slicing needs. I can slice cheese and mushrooms, fine grate or microplane ginger and chocolate, or shred potatoes—all with one handy tool.

Immersion blender

I love the immersion blender we have at the restaurant, but it's a great big stainless machine with super sharp blades and a boat motor inside of it. However, the smaller versions designed for use at home have two problems. They can't smooth soup perfectly, nor can they make margaritas. Your blender will perform these tasks to a tee!

Food processor

A food processor takes up a lot of space and is a bear to clean. Your box grater and blender will fulfill all the functions this ungainly item can perform.

Coffee maker

The idea of fitting an electric coffee maker on my counter is truly funny. Guests do deserve a good cup of coffee, and, interestingly enough, the tool that makes the tastiest cup is also the most CLK friendly. Get yourself a French press, and not only will you have the most flavorful cup of coffee in two minutes flat but cleanup will be a snap, and you can even use it to brew tea.

Electric can opener

Trusty old handheld can openers are not only reliable in a power outage, but most of them double as a bottle opener. Ditching your electric can opener for a manual model is a wonderful example of trading up from a one-trick pony to a CLK-friendly device.

Toaster/toaster oven

Anything you can drop in a toaster you can toast in a pan over medium heat. Unlike in the toaster oven, you can toast that bagel with butter in that same sauté pan without drying it out.

Spice rack

Besides wasting precious counter or cabinet space, spice racks hold spices that lack flavor and punch. Get rid of the crusty jars of decade-old spices and buy spices only as you need them.

Salad spinner

Yes, it will get your lettuce incredibly dry, but do you really need a gadget for this purpose? Simply allow your washed salad greens to drain inside the strainer or steamer basket of your large stockpot. Toss them around a little or pat them dry with a paper towel to expedite the process.

It's Not What You Have, It's How You Use It

I cannot overemphasize that what's in your Crappy Little Kitchen has very little to do with the gourmet meals that come out of it. It's what you do with what you have that makes all the difference. Without hiring an architect or civil engineer, you can convert a genuine hovel into a lean and mean crappy little machine! Organization is the key.

Once you've purged the extraneous items from your CLK, it's time to evaluate your kitchen layout. Try to think as logically as possible. I keep my jar of long handled utensils on top of my refrigerator right next to my stove. When I'm cooking, I can easily grab the utensil I need because it is in full sight and within arm's reach. (It doesn't hurt that I am taller than my refrigerator, but it can still work for you, too.) Put the set of mixing bowls next to the flour and sugar. Your pots and pans should already be hanging overhead, Keep the salt and pepper right on the stove.

Just like us, cabinets need to be beautiful on the inside as well as out. In a CLK, cabinets have to work double time. Placing a lazy Susan inside a cabinet adds a ton of usable space. Now the crap that you had buried in the back can swivel quite easily to the front. With a few minor tweaks, you can enhance the space in your crappy little cabinets and drawers. Add some trays to the drawers to separate your utensils. Don't throw your back out crawling inside that cavernous, low to the ground cabinet, just install some rolling shelves. You can buy them at any home improvement store, and the shelves come with detailed instructions. If I can do it, anybody can do it.

Buy inexpensive wire wine glass and coffee mug racks that you can easily install beneath your cabinets. You can even store everyday dishes, glasses, or appliances on freestanding shelves. Keep the good china wrapped up and boxed in an out-of-reach place for the rare occasion when you use it. Remember, you don't need to store kitchen items in the kitchen. I store my good china at my Mom's house and I never feel guilty about it! Cookbooks make wonderful conversation pieces and have beautiful pictures, so I keep mine on a bookshelf in the living room.

Lots and lots of light, especially natural light, help to create the illusion of space. If you have a window in the kitchen, don't block the light with dark curtains or shades. Open the blinds and let the light shine in. For artificial light, use energy efficient lightbulbs to decrease the heat your bulbs pump into the kitchen, while increasing brightness. If your CLK doesn't have well-placed overhead lighting (and most don't), you can easily install extra lighting beneath the cabinets. Buy battery-operated lights that adhere to the underside of the cabinet with adhesive tape. Brighten your walls with a fresh coat of semigloss paint. Food splatters wipe off easily from the slick surface semigloss provides. A clean, white canvas on your kitchen walls will make the room look and feel open and roomy.

The CLK Pantry

Stock minimal pantry items for everyday use. Most CLKs don't have a real pantry area, so I recommend using at least part of one upper cabinet for staple dry goods. You can buy any other spices you need in small quantities, as they are needed, not only to maintain freshness, but also to take up less room. Many grocery stores sell loose items in what is often called the bulk section. Don't let the name dissuade you. You can buy spices, nuts, and grains in small quantities as needed—even as little as a tablespoon at a time.

The list below covers items used repeatedly in the recipes for this book. It is not intended as a comprehensive list of ingredients used in the book since you would need quite a large pantry, as well as fridge, to keep all the ingredients on hand. Not to mention, the recipes often benefit from fresh-bought ingredients. Saffron is used several times throughout *Gourmet Meals in Crappy Little Kitchens*, but for financial and quality reasons, only buy a pinch at a time whenever you need it. When making gourmet meals in Crappy Little Kitchens on the fly (as we say in the biz), I would consider the following items "non-refrigerated staples":

- Quality sea salt
- Pepper mill
- Red pepper flakes
- Ground cumin
- White pepper
- Bay leaf
- Yellow curry powder
- Smoked paprika
- Cayenne pepper
- Extra virgin olive oil

- Tabasco
- Honey (your favorite)
- Soy sauce
- Crushed, canned tomatoes (they're always in season!)
- Dried pasta (only keep one variety on hand to save space, and just pick your favorite)
- Whole wheat bread
- Canned chipotle in adobo sauce
- Brown or white rice (whichever you prefer)
- Panko (Japanese bread crumbs)
- Chicken stock (or vegetable stock if you prefer)
- Kalamata olives
- Roma tomatoes
- Good vinegar (your favorite, but I use a lot of balsamic)
- Cornstarch
- Flour
- Sugar
- Powdered sugar
- Cornmeal
- Baking powder/baking soda
- Red wine (a chef's kitchen should always have alcohol!)
- Nutmeg and cinnamon (for desserts, but also for making coffee special)
- Speaking of that, coffee and tea (it's just polite)

THE AGE OF VINEGAR MATTERS

"Good" vinegar should be aged, much like fine wine. Often it is infused with flavors such as herbs or spices, but it can also be distilled from something other than grapes, like tomatoes, for example. Some specialty shops will actually pour tastings for you to try the wide variety of special vinegars available, and you won't get tipsy!

- Dark chocolate (70 percent cocoa concentration. Don't go any higher or it will taste very bitter. I find the chips or chunks melt very well, bake perfectly into cookies, and make a wonderful late night snack.)
- Quick cooking oats

Everything in Its Place

Now in my CLK, I keep a highly organized mini-pantry, which is actually just the cabinet next to the stove. Here's my functional arrangement:

Consider what you'll use most and keep it out. I use my sea salt, pepper mill, and olive oil every day, so I keep them out on the counter by my stove. Items that don't get used daily can go in the cabinet. Place pastas, rice, and beans toward the back, because they stack well and will probably be used once or twice a week at the most. Group together baking ingredients such as flour, sugar, baking soda, and baking powder and store them near the back.

Frequently used, but non-staple items sit in the first row or on a lazy Susan, if you have one. In my CLK that means pepper flakes, paprika, soy sauce, Tabasco, and honey.

Since most refrigerated items are perishable, buy them very close to the day you plan to consume them. You'll find very little inside a chef's refrigerator that doesn't come in a bottle or can, but I try to keep these items on hand for everyday use and in the event of pop-in guests.

- Eggs
- Butter
- Cream (for coffee)
- Yellow onions
- Beer and white wine (for guests and the chef—W. C. Fields said, "I love cooking with wine. Sometimes I even put it in the food.")
- Wedge of your favorite salty cheese (Hard salty cheeses last longer than soft or triple cream cheeses. Buy soft cheeses when you know someone is coming over.)
- Section of salami (If it gets around that you offer wine, cheese, and salami to the pop-ins . . . you'll be beating off friends with that stick of salami!)

Preventing Crappy Little Casualties

It's tough enough to maneuver as one person in a Crappy Little Kitchen. Have you ever experienced the excruciating pain of smacking the top of your head on the corner of an open cabinet or, heaven forbid, of sloshing scalding hot water on your arm? Throw one or two more cooks into the mix and accidents are bound to happen. The yelling you may hear that wafts into the dining room of your favorite restaurant probably comes from cooks giving a "heads up" in a professional kitchen to prevent such mishaps. Now in your CLK, there's no reason to yell, but you can apply the same principal to prevent crappy communication.

- When carrying something hot announce it. "Hot! Coming through." Your sous chef will know where you are and that you have something hot, so he'll get out of the way.
- When moving from one end of the kitchen to another, let everybody know. "Coming down!" This helps to prevent crappy little collisions.
- If you're working behind someone, make yourself known. "Behind you!" If he knows you're there, he won't turn around quickly and burn you with a hot sauté pan or accidentally turn into your knife.
- While carrying your knife through the kitchen, hold it down at your side and pointed directly at the ground, just as you learned to carry a scissor in grade school. Safety should come first when maneuvering around your CLK with a deadly weapon!
- Exercise common sense. Let your crouching kitchen partner know you just opened the cabinet above them. Make the kitchen a no-run zone (even running in small circles, which is all you can probably do, should be verboten). If you pull a pan out of the oven and set it on the counter, announce that it is "Hot!" so your friend won't try to pick it up.

Nine Gourmet Rules

Now that your CLK is well stocked, looks great, and has functional flow—what about taste? Remember a kitchen does not make a gourmet, but rather a gourmet makes the food that comes out of the kitchen. With a little practice, a few golden gourmet rules, and my restaurant-tested recipes and chef-wisdom, you'll possess the know-how to create beautiful and tasty culinary masterpieces from your Crappy Little Kitchen.

Rule number one: Buy fresh, seasonal, local, and organic. Purchasing seasonal fruits and veggies, not only ensures the best flavor and color, but it also saves money. Ask the produce person at the grocery store to point you in the direction of his freshest items. Buy local produce at farmer's markets and mom and pop grocers. When at the supermarket look for the country of origin on your fruits and veggies, and gravitate to products grown in your own region or state. Free range, vegetarian chickens without hormones, pesticide free peppers and tomatoes, and 100 percent whole grains will present you with a completely new spectrum of colors, flavors, and textures.

They don't make specialists for nothing! Purchase your meat from a butcher's shop, your fish from a seafood supplier, your produce, herbs, spices, eggs, and dairy from a farmer's market. You'll be pleased, not only with the quality and value of these products, but the people who work at these places remember faces and names and can offer great advice and ideas for the foods you are purchasing. I make a point of being friendly with specialty shop owners and workers. They can provide a plethora of information, from special deals you should jump at, to the freshest ingredients available, and they'll sometimes throw a little extra your way and won't let you buy anything you'll regret.

Rule number two: Before you do anything, always read a recipe through. This will make it easier to come up with a game plan and then a shopping list. You don't want to start cooking only to realize you don't have all necessary supplies, or that you don't have the time needed to cook the recipe start to finish. Make a list of all the ingredients you need to purchase including the specific amount desired, and shop for only two to three days at a time.

Rule number three: Get to know recipe lingo. If you want to cook like a chef, you need to learn some basic recipe terminology. Here's most of what you'll need to know to cook like a pro. According to American Culinary Federation guidelines, **chopping** results in random, irregular shaped pieces and has little to do with the size. **Dicing** involves cutting into uniform sizes and shapes. **Large dice** means a three-fourth-inch cube, **medium dice** means a one-half-inch cube, and small dice means a one-fourth-inch cube. A **brunois** is a one-eighth-inch cube. **Mincing** is anything smaller than a brunois. It is usually so fine that the product is almost pastelike.

Simmering is cooking at a lower temperature than boiling. This is when small bubbles may break at the surface, but they can be stirred down. Boiling takes place over higher heat with the liquid in full motion where large bubbles form, continuously break at the surface, and cannot be stirred down.

Folding usually involves using a rubber spatula to integrate two mixtures gently together without beating, to preserve the volume. You carefully cut down through one side of the mixture and then roll your spatula over, turning the bowl with each stroke, to "fold" the two together.

Sweating is the process of releasing flavors with moisture at a low temperature. Add a little olive oil and the vegetables to the sauté pan on low to medium heat. Cook for only a few minutes to release the moisture from the vegetables, but no browning should take place.

Rule number four: Prior to grocery shopping, take the time to check out what's already in the refrigerator. If you have leftovers, see if they can be used in your upcoming recipes, and throw away anything that's about to go bad. Rather than buying more tomatoes to dice in your Tomato and Avocado Frittata, use your leftover Pico de Gallo from the night before.

Rule number five: Break down your groceries right when you get home. I always have a box of quart-size and gallon-size freezer bags on hand for this purpose. That way, I can wrap all my fresh herbs in clean paper towels and put them in the same large bag. I separate my protein into usable portion sizes and put them in small bags, and my vegetables stay fresh longer in a sturdy plastic freezer bag than in the flimsy plastic sack intended for travel.

To save time when you're in a hurry, buy food that's already been cleaned and prepped for you. I frequent grocery store salad bars for perfectly sliced onion, carrot, and celery in whatever quantities my recipe calls for, and conveniently priced by the pound. Not only does this save you prep and cleanup time at home, but often the price per pound at the salad bar costs less than some vegetables whole, especially when you factor in what gets thrown away from waste.

Rule number six: Complete all the legwork before you start cooking. In a professional kitchen a chef will tell you to "mise en place" a recipe, which is French for "in its place." That means dice all your veggies (if you didn't buy them precut) and chop up the meat before you heat a pan. Pull out all the condiments for the recipe so you know you don't have to go digging for the flour while your garlic burns in the pan. A very CLK friendly concept since we might only be working from one cutting board.

Rule number seven: Always taste your food before you serve it. I will repeatedly ask you to season to taste with salt and pepper. Seasoning is a very personal preference. Only your taste buds can decide how much to add. Taste the dish first with no additional seasoning. If it tastes bland, add some salt, a pinch at a time, until the salt brings out the flavor of the food. You want to enhance the flavor of the food, not taste the salt. Move on with the pepper and do the same thing. Most important, never serve a dish that you haven't tasted, seasoned, and tasted again.

A few recipes call for you to season the meat heavily or liberally with salt and pepper. To do this, I want you to coat the food thoroughly with salt and pepper until the spices fall off the meat. The seasonings infuse the meat with flavor and enhance the overall depth of the dish. On the other hand, a recipe that says to season lightly means to sprinkle a pinch of salt and pepper over the whole dish.

Rule number eight: Presentation counts. For each recipe, I will provide you with step-by-step instructions on how to create an elaborate-looking plate with your limited space and resources. Use my ideas as a springboard for your own creativity, because a plate is like a blank canvas for you to paint your own stroke of genius. When developing your style, start with innovative garnishes you find pleasing, such as the ones found in the Soup section, and move on to mastering simple Appetizers and Salads. The good news is that every recipe completed, not only brings you closer to culinary dominance, but closer to dinner!

Rule number nine: Keep a sink full of hot soapy water whenever tackling a big cooking endeavor, even if you have a dishwasher (I don't in my Crappy Little Kitchen). Wash as you go, freeing up the pots and pans you need to use more than once, and cutting the end cleanup time to no time flat! Never let the pile of dishes left after a meal spook you out of cooking from scratch again.

Tuck these rules in your back pocket, and get ready to embark on a culinary journey only your Crappy Little Kitchen can provide. Nurture the love and cherish the uniqueness and glory of your Crappy Little Kitchen space. With my help and your willingness, your Crappy Little Kitchen will serve as the centerpiece for great times, gourmet food, and countless memories. With each recipe you'll become a stronger cook, gaining confidence as a chef until, eventually, you won't need me to tell you what to do. You will master the art of cooking, and take pride in your CLK and the special aura it creates. You will love your Crappy Little Kitchen as I love mine. I guarantee it.

Let's hold off on the love fest and get down to the meat of the matter (pun intended) by experiencing the gourmet recipes that follow.

"A"-Game Appetizers

Hors d'oeuvre is the French word for appetizer and sounds a lot more, well, appetizing than appetizer. When was the last time you went to a party where the host served tasty tidbits beyond the mundane chips and salsa? Since you live with a Crappy Little Kitchen, no one would expect more of you. However, these recipes are designed to work for you in your CLK. It's not the crappy old dart board, pool table, or card game that brings friends over to your parties . . . it's the food!

The French can make anything sound extraordinary, so at your next dinner party you can throw around the term

I guarantee your guests will be impressed and come back for more! Everything else will be crappy in comparison.

amuse bouche (pronounced uh-MYUZ-boosh), meaning "mouth amuser," which is a tiny morsel of food sent to a table before the meal. Whether you serve a formal meal or host a casually passed-hors d'oeuvre party, my recipes represent an excellent showcase for the artistry and showmanship of a chef under the worst of kitchen circumstances.

Shuttupahyourface Bruschetta

Serves 15

Bruschetta is by far the most CLK-friendly canapé out there. Make sure to use freshly grated Parmigiano-Reggiano, a true Parmesan cheese, which is one of the best cheeses in the world. Find it in a gourmet market and freshly grate it. A small wedge of gourmet cheese takes up far less room in your crappy little fridge than a big plastic container of inferior cheese that was grated, heaven knows when.

1 French baguette, thinly sliced

Extra virgin olive oil, as needed

3 garlic cloves (1 whole, 2 minced)

4 Roma tomatoes, small dice

5 basil leaves, thinly sliced

¼ cup finely grated Parmigiano-Reggiano cheese

Sea salt, to taste

Black pepper, to taste

1 Preheat your oven to 400°. Lay the baguette slices flat on a baking sheet, and drizzle lightly with the olive oil. Bake them in the oven for 10 to 15 minutes or until they are golden brown. Once cool, rub the whole garlic clove on each crostini.

Did You Know This Crap?

In Italian, the word crostini (pronounced kroh-STEE-nee) means little toasts. You can easily make these gourmet treats by toasting thin slices of bread, drizzling them with olive oil, and serving them warm. They may be topped with a savory, finely diced mixture such as cheese, vegetables, meat, or seafood.

2 In a bowl, combine the minced garlic, tomato, basil, Parmigiano-Reggiano cheese, and 3 tablespoons of extra virgin olive oil. The flavors of the tomato and basil will be brighter at room temperature, so allow the mixture to rest 5 minutes. Season with salt and pepper. Don't make the bruschetta topping too far in advance, or the basil will become droopy and look unappealing.

3 Carefully spoon a heaping tablespoon onto your crostini, and arrange them on a serving platter or tray. Assemble right before serving, or your bread will become soggy. Place any unused crostini in an airtight plastic bag or container where they'll stay crisp for three to five days.

Chefology

PARMIGIANO-REGGIANO

This pungent cheese has been crafted by Italian artisans for the past 800 years. Each wheel of Parmigiano-Reggiano carries proof of its authenticity in its rind. The number of the *caseificio*, which is the Italian word for cheese house, along with the production date with pin dots forming the words "Parmigiano-Reggiano" guarantee that it is real Parmigiano-Reggiano.

Get Stoked for Artichokes

Serves 10

Try making this appetizer while a couple of your friends look on. Even put them to work! It's not only a tremendously fun group activity, your friends will thank you for what they learned and will make the recipe for years to come.

2 red bell peppers

3 tablespoons extra virgin olive oil

5 large artichokes, whole and fresh

Sea salt as needed

2 lemons, cut in half

1 teaspoon minced garlic

Black pepper, to taste

3 tablespoons chopped Italian parsley

Chefology

JULIENNE
An essential skill for any chef, the French method of julienne means slicing vegetables into uniform-size matchsticks.

1 Preheat your oven to 500°. At this time, fill a 12-quart stockpot half way with water, and put it on high heat. Place the bell peppers on a baking sheet and drizzle with olive oil. Roast them in the oven for 15 to 20 minutes or until they begin to blacken and blister. Remove them and place them in a mixing bowl, cover with plastic wrap, and set aside. The peppers will steam themselves.

2 While you wait for the water to boil, cut off the top one-third of the artichokes and discard. Now, just as if you were shucking corn, peel off the dark coarse outer leaves until you reach the tender and pale greenish ones. Turn over the artichoke and trim off the dry green outer layer of the stem, then use a spoon to scoop out the inedible coarse purple flower or "choke" from the center of the artichoke.

3 Your water should be about to boil so add 2 tablespoons of sea salt to it, squeeze the lemons into the water and drop them right in. When the water comes to a boil, add the artichokes, reduce to a simmer, cover, and allow them to cook for about 25 minutes. When the bottom of the artichoke is tender, it's done cooking. After 25 minutes, test one by removing it from the water and piercing it with a fork.

If it pierces easily, it's ready. Drain the artichokes and allow them to cool. Discard the water and lemons.

4 When the peppers have cooled, pull off their tops, turn them upside down, and allow the seeds and juices to drain. Carefully peel off their skins. (Do not rinse them because you'll lose so much flavor that way!) Once they are peeled, slice them into slender julienne and put them in a medium-size bowl. Add the minced garlic, and season to taste with salt and pepper.

5 Return to your cooled artichokes, and peel off and discard all the leaves until you reach the heart. You'll know you've reached the heart when you see what looks and feels like a soft, yet solid, yellow core. Cut all the hearts in half horizontally, and then in half again horizontally to create slices. If you'd like to turn this recipe into a side dish, leave the hearts in half to create larger portions.

6 Spoon a heaping tablespoon of the pepper mixture on top of an artichoke heart slice. Garnish each one with a little chopped fresh parsley, and arrange in a circular pattern on a platter. Serve at room temperature.

Did You Know This Crap?

To simmer is to cook at a lower temperature than boiling—when small bubbles may break at the surface, but they can be stirred down. Boiling takes place over higher heat with the liquid in full motion where large bubbles form, continuously break at the surface, and cannot be stirred down.

• • • • • • • • • • • • •

Artichokes are not vegetables; they are actually flower buds and members of the sunflower family. Select artichokes with uniform color, and undamaged, tightly closed leaves. Smaller artichokes have more tender leaves (the leaves of baby artichokes are entirely edible); larger ones have bigger hearts.

Look-Like-You-Didn't-Hurry Curry Chicken Salad

Serves 15

Always a crowd-pleaser, this is an appetizer filled with complex flavors and textures, yet so easy and inexpensive to prepare. Look for small square loaves of presliced "party bread" that can be cut into triangles, buttered, and toasted to save time on this recipe.

Sea salt, as needed

6 boneless, skinless chicken thighs

1 pumpernickel, sourdough, or French baguette, thinly sliced

½ cup melted butter

¼ cup chopped dried cherries

¼ cup chopped and toasted pecans

¼ cup real mayonnaise (not "mayonnaise dressing" or Miracle Whip)

3 tablespoons yellow curry powder

1½ tablespoons mango chutney

Black pepper, to taste

Small handful fresh dill, small sprigs

1 Preheat oven to 400°. Fill a 12-inch sauté pan halfway with water, and set it on high heat. When it begins to simmer, add 3 tablespoons of sea salt and let it dissolve. Trim the fat off the chicken thighs.

2 Place the bread slices on a sheet tray. Using a pastry brush, lightly coat them with the melted butter, and bake for 10 to 15 minutes or until they are crispy crostini.

3 When the water comes to a boil, turn the heat down to medium. Using tongs, gently

Swap It

FOR PEOPLE with less discerning palates—say, a group of kids—replace the dried cherries with red, seedless grapes, and the pumpernickel with graham crackers.

How to Toast Nuts

Every gourmet chef knows the trick to tastier nuts is to toast them. Toasting nuts not only brings out their natural flavors but also makes chopping them a breeze. The best part about toasting nuts is it is so simple to do and yet provides outstanding results. Throw your nuts in a dry skillet over medium heat and cook until they are golden brown. Alternatively, spread the nuts on a sheet tray and bake in a 350° oven for 10 to 15 minutes.

set the thighs into the water. Simmer for exactly 10 minutes, then remove them and place them in a medium-size bowl and cover with ice for 5 minutes to stop their cooking. Then drain and roughly chop the chicken into bite-size pieces, and return it to the bowl.

4 Add the cherries, pecans, mayonnaise, curry powder, and mango chutney, and toss gently. Season to taste with salt and pepper.

5 Carefully spoon a heaping table-spoon onto each crostini right before serving to avoid soggy-bread syndrome. Then garnish each piece with a sprig of dill and arrange them on a platter or serving tray. Store leftover crostini in an airtight plastic bag or container.

Did You Know This Crap?

I've worked for chefs who prefer curry paste to curry powder. However, for this application, I prefer using the freshly ground curry powder I get at my farmer's market. Just like pepper, when the spices in curry are ground up, they begin to lose the essential oils that flavor them. Ask the spice purveyor at your farmer's market when the curry was made. If it has been made in the last three days, and you plan on cooking with it today, you're in good shape. If you use curry paste, start with one-half tablespoon because some brands are extremely salty.

No-Space Meatballs

Serves 15

Because we "fry" these meatballs directly on a tray in the oven, they require no sauté pan, making the dish a one-pan wonder! The only risk you run with this recipe is not making enough.

8 ounces ground pork

8 ounces ground veal

½ cup finely grated Manchego cheese, plus more shaved for garnish

¼ cup finely chopped flat leaf parsley

3 tablespoons finely chopped fresh sage

3 garlic cloves, minced

1 large egg

1 cup fine bread crumbs

3 tablespoons white wine

1 teaspoon sea salt

½ teaspoon black pepper

2 tablespoons olive oil

1 cup Spicy Pomodoro Sauce (p. 211)

1 Place the pork, veal, cheese, parsley, sage, and garlic in a medium bowl, then add the egg, bread crumbs, white wine, salt, and pepper. Using clean hands, gently fold the ingredients together, without overworking it. Now, form meatballs about one inch in diameter. Place them one-half inch apart on a sheet tray that

Swap It

MANCHEGO is a very popular Spanish cheese with a full, rich flavor and a healthy dose of sharpness. Mahon, a more adventuresome Spanish cheese alternative imparts a distinctive flavor with its olive oil and paprika infused rind. You might want to try idiazabal (eee-dee-ya-ZA-bal), which has a rich taste and perfumed aroma, and stands out as the quintessential cheese made from sheep's milk. If Spanish cheeses are scarce in your neck of the woods, just use a nice salty Parmesan.

Crappy Little Kitchens

Tomatoes

Purchase tomatoes only a day or so before you plan to use them, and never refrigerate them. The cold ruins their flavor and makes their flesh turn mealy. Display the bright red orbs in the wire baskets you have hanging from the ceiling. Tomatoes will never take up space in your crappy little fridge again.

you drizzled with olive oil and then spread with a pastry brush. Chill the meatballs overnight or for at least one hour to set them up, which in chef terms means to become firm.

2 Preheat oven to 450°. Bake the meatballs for ten minutes and then rotate the pan to bake for another 5 to 10 minutes or until golden brown.

3 To serve, arrange the meatballs on your serving tray and insert a toothpick at 3 o'clock (slightly askew). Top with a teaspoon of Spicy Pomodoro Sauce and a single shaving of Manchego cheese.

Did You Know This Crap?

Italian or flat leaf parsley has more flavor than curly parsley and is therefore preferred for cooking. Don't ever opt for dried parsley because it has no flavor at all. Look for bright green leaves that show no sign of wilting. When you get it home, rinse it off, wrap it in a paper towel, and store it in a plastic bag in your fridge. It will last for about a week.

Greek-Godlike
Stuffed Tomatoes

Stuff the tomatoes and place them on your baking sheet before the guests arrive, so all you'll need to do is pop them in the oven. Very CLK friendly.

8 Roma tomatoes, thumb size

Freshly cracked pepper, to taste

6 tablespoons extra virgin olive oil (divided in two)

1 cup feta cheese

¼ cup chopped Italian parsley

¼ cup chopped Kalamata olives

1 tablespoon minced garlic

8 romaine lettuce leaves

1 Preheat oven to 350°. Thinly slice off the very top and bottom of the tomatoes (only enough to make a flat surface), and then cut them in half right through the waist. Using a measuring spoon, carefully scoop out the insides—don't scoop too deeply—to make sixteen tomato cups.

2 Lightly pepper the inside of the tomatoes and evenly drizzle with 3 tablespoons of olive oil. In a small bowl, gently combine the feta cheese, parsley, olives, and garlic. Stuff the cheese mixture into the tomato cups. Lightly pepper the top of each cup.

3 Use the remaining 3 tablespoons of olive oil to grease a small sheet tray and arrange the stuffed tomatoes on the oiled surface. Bake for 15 to 20 minutes or until the cheese begins to brown. Line your platter or serving tray with the romaine spears (you can cut through the middle rib to make them lay flat on your tray), and arrange your stuffed tomatoes over the top. Serve immediately.

Bloody Good Tomatoes

Serves 10

Don't just save these marinated tomatoes for appetizers. This recipe holds up well to pasta and tastes great tossed with squares of toasted day-old bread for a salad. You can also heat it up and pour it over a juicy steak. Try making it a day ahead of serving, so the delicious flavors have a chance to blend.

3 tablespoons balsamic vinegar

1 tablespoon Worcestershire sauce

¼ cup extra virgin olive oil

1 pint red grape tomatoes

1 pint yellow pear tomatoes

1 small red onion, diced

8 garlic cloves, crushed

1 teaspoon crushed red pepper

Sea salt, to taste

Pepper, to taste

Celery sticks, thin cut, about 2 inches long, for garnish

1 Pour balsamic vinegar and Worcestershire sauce into a medium bowl. While whisking vigorously, slowly drizzle in the olive oil, making a light dressing. Add the tomatoes, onion, garlic, and red pepper. Season to taste with salt and pepper. Cover tightly and allow it to sit in the refrigerator overnight.

2 Bring the bowl out an hour before serving to allow tomatoes to come to room temperature. Arrange shot glasses on your serving tray and fill them ¾ cup of the way up with the marinated tomatoes. Add celery stick to use as a utensil. No forks needed!

Fried Green Tomatoes

Reserve one hand for dipping the tomato slices in the dry ingredients and one hand for the wet ingredients, which will keep one hand free of the messy bread-crumb coating. Putting your sheet tray on the stove next to the pan of oil will save on much-needed counter space when tackling this recipe!

1 cup olive oil blend, (part olive oil and part canola or vegetable oil to increase smoke point)

4 green tomatoes, largest available

Sea salt, to taste

Black pepper, to taste

2 cups all-purpose flour

2 tablespoons ground cumin

1 tablespoon turmeric

1 tablespoon smoked Spanish paprika, plus more for garnish

1 tablespoon garlic powder

2 cups buttermilk

3 eggs

2 cups panko, Japanese bread crumbs

2 ounces Manchego cheese

1 Put your 12-inch sauté pan on the stove at medium high heat. Add the oil and allow it to heat for at least 8 minutes before testing it. Set a sheet tray lined with paper towels on the two (unlit) burners next to the sauté pan.

2 Slice your tomatoes into ¼-inch disks (you should get about four per tomato) and season each side liberally with salt and pepper.

3 Line up three shallow bowls. In the first one, combine the flour, cumin, turmeric, paprika, and garlic powder and mix them well with a whisk. In the second bowl, whisk together the buttermilk and eggs. Dump the panko bread crumbs in the last bowl.

4 Throw a few crumbs of panko into the oil and if they immediately pop and fry, the oil is ready.

5 Coat four of the tomato slices in the seasoned flour and shake off any excess. Then dip them in the buttermilk mixture and then panko. Gently set the breaded tomatoes into the oil and allow them to fry on one side while you prepare four more tomato slices. Once the bottoms of the first batch of frying

tomatoes are golden brown, turn them over to cook on the other side.

6 Line a sheet tray with paper towels. When the tomatoes are golden brown all over, remove them from the oil and place them on paper towels to drain. Allow 1 minute for the oil to come back up to temperature and use this time to prepare the rest of the tomatoes for frying. Then fry the next batch, and so on.

7 Arrange the fried green tomatoes on a platter, and then use your vegetable peeler to slice the Manchego over the top. Garnish with a dusting of smoked Spanish paprika, and serve immediately.

Swap It

I like to use a mild Spanish cheese like Manchego in this recipe, but if you prefer a good Parmesan (made from cow's milk) or Pecorino (this one is made from sheep's milk), go with that.

Great Guacamole, Batman!

Serves
10

Many versions of guacamole contain primarily avocado and have a somewhat creamy and chunky texture, but I like making a guacamole and Pico de Gallo combination, which is an avocado and tomato-based recipe.

2 large ripe avocados

½ cup medium-diced red onion

½ cup medium-dice Roma tomato

1 jalapeno, small dice

2 garlic cloves, minced

1 lime, juiced

Sea salt, to taste

Pepper, to taste

1 Dicing an avocado need not be messy and is actually a very CLK friendly process. Rather than scooping the avocado pulp out onto the cutting board to dice it, each avocado is diced while inside it's skin. Then it pops directly into its bowl with no muss and even less fuss! Cut the avocado in half by running your knife around the pit and then twisting the two halves apart. Gently tap the blade of your knife into the pit, twist, and the pit will pop right out, still attached to your blade. Set your avocado cut side up on your cutting board and, without breaking through the outer skin, slice a grid pattern into the flesh of the avocado. Scoop out the diced avocado using a large spoon and place it in a medium bowl. Repeat with the other avocado.

2 In that same bowl, gently fold in the rest of the ingredients. Try to maintain the shape of the diced avocado. Season to taste with salt and pepper. Lay plastic wrap directly on the spread, cover tightly, and refrigerate until you are ready to use. You should serve this within a few hours or your top layer of avocado will become brown from oxidation.

3 Serve inside a premade tortilla shell bowl along with a variety of (all natural) colorful tortilla corn chips for a vibrant display.

Did You Know This Crap?

Avocados are actually a fruit, not a vegetable.

Bloody Mary Bloody Mary Bloody Mary Relish!

Serves 10

For a chic party treat, spread bite-size celery spears with this relish or fill chilled martini glasses with it, and serve with poached shrimp around the rim for an adults-only version of shrimp cocktail! Any way you present it, it comes together as a one-bowl wonder!

2 Roma tomatoes, small dice

1 celery stalk, small dice

1 garlic clove, minced

2 scallions, thinly sliced

3 tablespoons tomato juice

2 teaspoons Worcestershire sauce

Tabasco sauce, to taste

2 teaspoons jarred horseradish

1 teaspoon vodka

1 lemon, juiced

Sea salt, to taste

Pepper, to taste

Celery, 10 two-inch sticks

1 In a medium bowl, combine the tomato, celery, garlic, and all but 2 tablespoons of scallions. Add the tomato juice, Worcestershire, and Tabasco according to how spicy you like your Bloody Mary. Feel free to make this up to two days in advance, but don't add the ingredients of step 2 until the day it will be served.

2 Stir in the horseradish, vodka, and lemon juice. Season to taste with salt and pepper. Cover tightly and refrigerate, if you aren't going to serve it immediately.

3 Serve in chilled tumbler glasses with celery sticks, garnished with the remaining scallions.

Above-and-Beyond Spinach and Artichoke Dip with Hawaiian Bread

Serves 15

Everyone has seen a version of this dip served in a loaf of sourdough bread, but my friend Amy Taylor is the one who told me to put my spectacular spinach dip in a loaf of Hawaiian bread. Pure genius. With no serving bowl to clean afterward, your crappy little sink will thank you.

3 tablespoons extra virgin olive oil

16 ounces artichoke hearts, canned

¼ cup minced garlic (about 6 cloves)

1 pound fresh baby spinach

½ cup heavy cream

¼ cup shredded Pecorino cheese

Sea salt, to taste

Pepper, to taste

1 loaf Hawaiian bread, round

1 Preheat oven to 350°. Put your 12-inch sauté pan over medium heat, and allow it to heat for 5 minutes. Add the olive oil to the pan, and again allow it to heat for 5 minutes.

2 Buy quartered artichoke hearts or quarter the whole ones lengthwise. Using your tongs, carefully add them to the hot pan and arrange them to cover the bottom of the pan evenly. Let them cook in the pan without moving them for 8 minutes, to brown them on one side.

3 Add the garlic and spinach, and fold the mixture to wilt the spinach. You may need to add the spinach a small amount at a time. (Once wilted, everything will fit in the sauté pan perfectly.)

4 Add the heavy cream and turn down the heat slightly to allow the cream to reduce and thicken for 10 minutes, stirring occasionally. Stir in the cheese. Season to taste with salt and pepper.

5 While it is thickening, use your bread knife to carve out the center of the Hawaiian bread, making it into a bowl, and saving the

bread cap. Place it on one side of a baking sheet. Cut the bread cap into ½-inch cubes and arrange them on the other side of the baking sheet. When the dip is thick, pour it into the bread bowl, and place the baking sheet in the oven. Bake for 10 to 15 minutes or until the bread is crisp and the dip is brown over the top.

6 Serve immediately. Carefully place the bowl in the center of a platter, surrounded by the toasted bread cubes. Remember that the gourmet chef gets to eat the bowl. You can, but why not share with your friends, and let them tear up the yummy bowl?

Did You Know This Crap?

Having a sweet taste and light texture, King's Hawaiian Sweet Bread is available at most grocery stores in a round, uncut loaf. If you can't find this bread in your area, try baking your own. You don't need any special equipment, and homemade bread screams gourmet.

Yield: 3 round loaves

To make homemade Hawaiian bread follow this easy recipe:

3 eggs

1 cup pineapple juice

1 cup water

¾ cup sugar

½ teaspoon ground ginger

1 teaspoon vanilla extract

1 teaspoon sea salt

4 ounces unsalted butter, melted

6½ cups all-purpose flour

3 tablespoons instant active yeast

1 Beat the eggs, pineapple juice, water, sugar, ginger, vanilla, salt, and melted butter in a large mixing bowl. Add 3 cups of flour to the egg mixture and stir until well mixed. Sprinkle in yeast, 1 tablespoon at a time, mixing well. Gradually add the other 3 cups of flour. The batter will be hard to mix with a spoon. You may have to use your hand.

2 Make sure it's mixed well. Leave the batter in a bowl and cover with the cloth and put it in a warm place. Let it rise 1 hour. Remove the dough from the bowl and knead in ½ cup more flour. Knead about 10 times. Divide the dough into 3 equal parts and place it in well-greased round cake pans. Cover and put it in a warm place and let rise about 1 hour. Bake at 350° for 20 to 30 minutes.

Crabtastic Avocado Cakes

Serves 25

No gourmet chef's repertoire is complete without a knock-your-socks-off crab cake recipe. And this is the one. Because these crab cakes are "fried" in the oven, we only need to use our sauté pan once. Form the cakes and freeze them up to three days before your party, and they'll be ready to pop in the oven right before your guests arrive.

3 ripe avocados, large

2 limes, juiced

6 tablespoons extra virgin olive oil

1 cup small diced yellow onion

3 garlic cloves, minced

1 inch piece of fresh ginger, minced

¼ cup small diced red bell pepper

1 jalapeno, small dice with most seeds removed

3 tablespoons unsalted butter

½ cup bread crumbs

½ cup heavy cream

2 eggs

1 pound lump crabmeat

1 pound select crabmeat

Sea salt, to taste

Pepper, to taste

1 cup Chipotle Aioli (p. 198)

2 limes, thinly sliced

1 Prepare the avocado as described on page 40 and place it in a large bowl with the lime juice. Set aside.

2 Put your 12-inch sauté on medium heat. Add 3 tablespoons of olive oil and allow it to heat up. Sauté the onion, garlic, ginger, bell pepper, and jalapeno together until the onions are translucent, about 8 minutes. Add the butter and allow it to melt. Add the bread crumbs and allow them to toast in the butter while absorbing the moisture from the vegetables. Add the cream and turn off the heat while stirring. Fold in the eggs quickly to temper them (brings the eggs slowly up to the temperature of the cream which keeps them from scrambling when the crab cakes bake in the oven.

3 Add the sautéed mixture to the bowl of avocado. Gently fold in the crabmeat, trying to maintain the shape of the lump crab and avocado. Season to taste with salt and pepper. Using your ⅛ measuring cup (you should get approximately 50 to 60 cakes), portion out the crab mix onto a sheet tray lined with wax paper, wrap tightly with plastic wrap, and put into the freezer for 30 minutes. Once frozen, you can

pop them into a freezer bag and freeze for up to 3 days.

4 Preheat your oven to 500°. Using your pastry brush, spread 3 tablespoons of olive oil on a baking sheet and evenly space the frozen crab cakes ½-inch apart. Put them in the oven to brown for 15 minutes and then rotate the pan to roast another 10 to 15 minutes or until golden brown.

5 Arrange the lime slices on your platter or serving tray, and set a warm crab cake on each slice, and add a small dot of chipotle aioli on each cake. Serve immediately.

Chefology

CRABMEAT

Lump crabmeat represents the whole pieces of the white body meat, while select meat is small bits of light and dark meat from the body and claws. When it comes to crabmeat, you want to keep all the lumps intact, while removing all the shells. Use your clean hands to gently sort through the crabmeat. Don't shred the meat while you do this, but gently squeeze the bits between your thumb and index finger to detect any small broken bits of shell and remove them.

For a Good Time Call . . .
Champagne Oysters

Serves
6

As bold a statement that oysters make, this recipe is incredibly CLK friendly. All you need is a butter knife, a dishtowel, a sheet tray, and a 1-quart saucepot.

1½ cups brut
  Champagne

3 tablespoons minced
  chives, plus 1 inch
  strips for garnish

12 fresh oysters

Rock salt, as needed

3 ounces unsalted
  butter

Sea salt, to taste

1 Preheat your oven to 400°. Heat a 1-quart saucepot over medium-high heat, and add the Champagne and chives, bringing them to a boil. Allow the liquid to evaporate until the Champagne has reduced by half.

2 While you wait for the liquid to reduce, place the shucked oysters on a sheet tray. If some of the shells are wobbly and uneven, level them out by putting a small pile of rock

Did You Know This Crap?

If you buy affordable Champagne, it's probably not a true Champagne at all, but rather a sparkling wine. Real Champagne is only produced within the Champagne region of France and comes with a steep price tag.

How to Shuck Oysters

Hold a thick dishtowel in the center of your weaker hand and use it as a cushion to grasp an oyster. The oyster's hinge should face the crook in your thumb and index finger. Take a butter knife (don't use anything sharper—you could easily cut yourself!), and insert the tip between the two shells against the little protrusion (it will look like a hinge). While applying firm pressure, wiggle the blade between the shells and pry them apart. Now take your paring knife and carefully separate the top shell and discard it. Run the knife along the bottom shell, cutting through the two muscles to free the oyster, but leave it (and its juices) in the shell. Repeat with the remaining oysters.

salt under them. Place the sheet tray in the oven and roast the oysters for five minutes. When removing them from the oven, be careful not to lose any of the juice inside the shells.

3 Turn the heat down to low on the reduced Champagne. Slowly (a tablespoon at a time) whisk the butter into the reduced Champagne. Then whisk quickly, to emulsify the butter and Champagne. Remove the saucepan from the heat and season to taste with salt.

4 Pour rock salt onto a serving tray and arrange the oysters on top. Spoon about a teaspoon of Champagne butter sauce over each oyster on the half shell, and top with a strip of chive at an angle over the oyster, like a sword. Serve immediately.

Scallops Ceviche

Serves 6 to 8

Ceviche is a perfect summertime entertaining appetizer. A popular dish in the warm coastal regions of South America, it is prepared in a centuries-old method of cooking seafood through its contact with the acidic juice of citrus instead of heat. Considering this recipe "cooks" itself in a disposable bag, well I just don't think it gets any more CLK friendly than that!

15 U-10 sea scallops

1 lime

1 cup freshly squeezed lime juice

2 garlic cloves, chopped

1 teaspoon red pepper flakes

Sea salt, to taste

15 scallop shells, scrubbed clean

½ cup thinly sliced shallots

3 tablespoons chopped cilantro

1 Remove the white muscle or "foot" from the side of each scallop. This is the slightly off-white flap on the side of the scallop, and it will peel off quite easily.

2 Zest the lime, and add the zest along with the lime juice, garlic, and red pepper flakes to a freezer bag, and then season to taste with salt. Add the sea scallops and make sure they are all immersed in the lime juice. Close tightly and refrigerate about 4 hours—but no longer than 8.

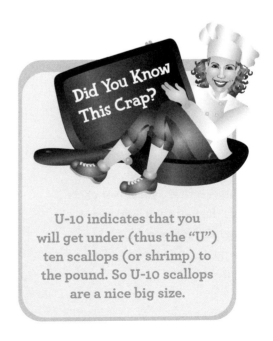

Did You Know This Crap?

U-10 indicates that you will get under (thus the "U") ten scallops (or shrimp) to the pound. So U-10 scallops are a nice big size.

How to Zest a Lime

Take a whole washed lime, and rub it up and down on the fine grating side of your box grater. You only want to zest the outer colored part of the lime peel because the white pith is bitter. Instead of using your box grater, you can use your vegetable peeler to slice off the colored peel then mince it with your chef's knife.

3 A few minutes before serving, place the scallop shells on your serving platter and set 1 scallop inside each shell. Dip the sliced shallots in the ceviche marinade to dress them, and place a pinch on top of each scallop. Garnish with the chopped cilantro and serve immediately.

Swap It

IF YOU'RE IN A HURRY, you can use bay scallops, which are small and need to marinate for only 30 minutes.

Hot-and-Bothered Dragonfly Prawns

Serves 10

Leave the tails on the shrimp, they serve as nifty handles for the appetizer, making the need for utensils (and washing them later) unnecessary.

¼ cup sea salt, plus more to taste for sauce

¼ cup granulated sugar

2 cups water

4 cups ice

20 medium prawns, peeled and deveined

3 tablespoons extra virgin olive oil, for oiling sheet tray

1 teaspoon cayenne pepper

1 cup cubed seedless watermelon

1 tablespoon honey

3 tablespoons prepared horseradish

3 lemons, sliced thin into 20 slices

1 small bunch cilantro

1 Preheat your oven to 300°. Add the ¼ cup of sea salt, sugar, and water to a 1-quart saucepan, and place over high heat. Simmer and stir until the sugar and salt are dissolved, then remove from heat. Add the ice to chill the brine (brine is simply salted water), and once cold, add the prawns and allow them to brine for 20 minutes.

2 Remove the prawns from the brine, pat dry with a clean towel, and put them on a lightly oiled baking sheet to keep them from

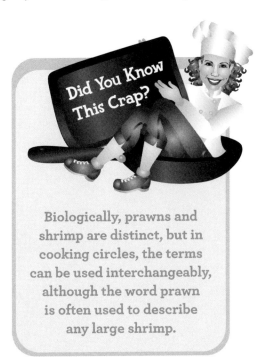

Did You Know This Crap?

Biologically, prawns and shrimp are distinct, but in cooking circles, the terms can be used interchangeably, although the word prawn is often used to describe any large shrimp.

How to Devein Shrimp

Pull off the head (if it is still attached) and legs. Starting with the head end, pull off the outer shell. For the purposes of this recipe, keep the last segment of shell and the tail tip on. Using a paring knife, cut along the outer edge of the shrimp's back, about ¼-inch deep. Remove and discard the vein that runs along the surface of the back.

• •

sticking. Lightly dust the prawns with cayenne and bake them for 4 minutes. Turn them over, allow them to cool on the pan, and then refrigerate them.

3 In your blender, combine the watermelon, honey, and horseradish and puree until smooth. Season to taste with salt. If you like your cocktail sauce spicier, add more horseradish.

4 Arrange the lemon slices on your platter or serving tray. Lay a prawn in the center of each lemon slice, with two cilantro leaves poking out from beneath like wings. Drizzle the cocktail sauce the length of the prawn and serve immediately.

Get Freaky Tzatziki
(tsah-ZEE-Kee)

Serves 12

This is a classic Greek yogurt and cucumber sauce that's light and refreshing and perfect to enjoy in hot weather.

1 English cucumber, ½ cup small dice and slice the rest of the cucumber into disks

4 scallions, sliced

1 garlic clove, minced

1 cup plain Greek yogurt

¼ cup chopped fresh mint

Sea salt, to taste

Pepper, to taste

4 whole wheat pitas, cut into wedges

1 Preheat your oven to 350°.

2 Combine the cucumber, scallions, garlic, yogurt, and mint in a small bowl. Season to taste with salt and pepper. Cover tightly and refrigerate up to two days in advance, freeing up lots of time and preparation space the day of your get-together (very CLK friendly)!

3 Put the pita wedges on a sheet tray and toast for 10 minutes.

4 To serve, place an ice-cold bowl of tzatziki in the center of a platter surrounded by warm pita chips and crisp cucumber chips.

Did You Know This Crap?

Choose an English or seedless cucumber, which is also known as burpless since it doesn't cause any intestinal distress. These cucumbers are wrapped in plastic and therefore ship and keep well. They don't require peeling so you can leave the skin intact for the beautiful green color and for less work in your CLK.

Superior Soups

Soups and Crappy Kitchens go hand in hand.

What could be easier than combining a crap load of ingredients into one big pot to create a delicious, nutritious meal? While soups are valued for the comfort they bring, they also showcase your talent as a chef. Many say the ability to make a well-executed soup is a true sign of an accomplished chef. Try your hand at these recipes, and you'll be on your way to gourmet chefdom.

I will show you how to up the ante on your soup-making game so your creations not only provide comfort but also tantalize your taste buds.

Most of my recipes make ten or more servings of soup. If you're not inviting over a crowd, I recommend freezing the leftovers in single serving containers that can be microwaved for a steaming hot gourmet meal in minutes! You'll get several delicious no-mess meals you and your CLK will love.

Sara's Dill Tomato Soup

This delicious recipe demonstrates how you can easily deviate from a traditional tomato soup recipe with spectacular results. Try your hand at being creative. Change your herbs, take out the cream to make it brighter, or add summer vegetables or even pasta. All-but-the-kitchen-sink cooking really finds itself at home in the Crappy Little Kitchen. Use up the leftovers in the fridge, by throwing them in the soup!

3 tablespoons extra
  virgin olive oil

3 tablespoons unsalted
  butter

2 yellow onions,
  chopped

1 garlic clove, smashed

Sea salt, to taste

Black pepper, to taste

¼ cup tomato paste

10 Roma tomatoes,
  chopped
  (may substitute
  30 ounces diced
  canned tomato)

15 ounces crushed
  tomato, canned

4 cups vegetable stock

½ cup chopped
  fresh dill

1 cup heavy cream

¼ cup quartered
  kalamata olives

1 In a 12-quart stockpot, heat the olive oil and butter over medium heat. After the butter has melted into the olive oil, add the onion and garlic, and allow them to sweat slowly. This is when the heat gently draws out

Chefology

KALAMATA OLIVES

A Greek almond-shaped olive, the kalamata has a dark eggplant color and a rich and fruity flavor. Because it is difficult to remove the pit without mangling the olive, buying pitted kalamatas saves a lot of time and frustration.

How to Smash Garlic

Place a clove of garlic on a flat cutting surface. Lay the side of your chef's knife blade (slanted with the sharp side toward the cutting board, not up) centered on the clove. With the heel of your free hand, give one swift smack to the portion of the blade centered over the clove. When you raise the knife, you'll notice the clove is pulverized and its paper skin will lift off easily.

moisture from the vegetables. Season lightly with salt and pepper. You want them to soften, not brown.

2 When the onions are translucent, add the tomato paste and allow it to melt evenly into the onions. Next, add the chopped tomatoes and crushed tomatoes, and cook for 10 to 15 minutes, stirring constantly. Add the vegetable stock and fresh dill, and bring the soup to a simmer. Turn the heat down slightly and allow the soup to cook slowly for 30 minutes. Stir often to prevent the soup from burning on the bottom.

3 Take the pot of soup off the heat, and, stirring constantly, drizzle in the heavy cream and season to taste with salt and pepper. Serve warm with a tablespoon of olives in the center of each bowl of soup.

Did You Know This Crap?

Chock full of vitamins C, A, and B, potassium, iron, and phosphorus, tomatoes make a mean pot of soup. I love to cook with and eat tomatoes. Most often I use Roma tomatoes because of their consistent quality, shape, flavor, texture, and good shelf life. Whenever canned tomatoes can be substituted, I'll note it in the recipe. With the possible exception of chocolate (although I've never tried the combination), I can't think of anything that doesn't blend well with tomato.

Gazpacho Margarita, Ole!

**Yields
3 quarts**
(10 servings)

The acid from citrus juice or vinegar gives traditional gazpacho that kick we savor, but I like to add tequila and lime juice to make it extra special. Anytime I can eat a beautiful healthy meal without turning on my stove, it . . . well, it turns me on!

1 English cucumber, medium dice

1 red onion, medium dice

6 Roma tomatoes, medium dice

1 green bell pepper, medium dice

1 jalapeno, seeded, small dice

2 garlic cloves, minced

40 ounces tomato juice

¼ cup extra gold tequila

⅓ cup fresh squeezed lime juice

¼ cup extra virgin olive oil

Sea salt, to taste

Black pepper, to taste

2 limes, cut into wedges

1 Mix all the ingredients together, except for the salt, pepper, and lime wedges, and chill for several hours until icy cold. Lightly puree half of the soup in a blender, and then add the rest and puree both portions together. Season to taste with salt and pepper.

2 Serve cold with a lime wedge propped on the rim of each bowl of soup.

Did You Know This Crap?

Gazpacho originated in the Andalusia region of southern Spain. Usually prepared from a pureed mixture of fresh tomatoes, sweet bell peppers, onions, celery, cucumber, bread crumbs, garlic, olive oil, vinegar, and sometimes lemon juice, gazpacho makes a perfect hot weather soup.

Tahitian-Style Corn and Crab Soup

Yields 2 quarts (6 servings)

If possible, you can grill the corn on the cob, but in my Crappy Little Kitchen, I just roast it, because grilling on a crappy little fire escape is illegal! Don't forget the squeeze of fresh lime at the end, it adds a spark of freshness to the finished product.

6 ears of corn, freshly shucked or 3 cups frozen corn kernels

3 tablespoons extra virgin olive oil

6 garlic cloves, chopped

6 shallots, chopped

1 stem lemongrass, smashed with your chef's knife

1 tablespoon peeled and grated fresh ginger

14 ounces lump crabmeat, save 6 nice size lumps for garnish

1 teaspoon shaved palm sugar or light brown sugar

4 cups vegetable stock

1 cup coconut milk, canned

Sea salt, to taste

Black pepper, to taste

2 limes, cut into wedges

1 Preheat your oven to 500°. Place your ears of corn on a sheet tray and roast them in the oven until all the kernels are bright yellow and some have begun to brown, about 10 to 15 minutes. Allow them to cool completely and remove the kernels. If you use frozen corn, place the kernels directly on the sheet tray and roast as above.

2 In a 12-quart stockpot, heat the olive oil over medium-high heat, and add the garlic, shallot, lemongrass, and ginger, stirring for 5 minutes. Add the roasted corn kernels, and, stirring often, allow the corn to cook for 15 minutes.

3 Add 12 ounces of crabmeat, palm sugar, vegetable stock, and coconut milk to the pot, and allow the mixture to come to a simmer. Reduce heat to medium and cook the soup for another 45 minutes. Remove the lemongrass.

4 Use your blender to puree the soup, and then strain the soup into a pot over low heat. You'll need to do this in batches. Discard what is left in the strainer. Season to taste with salt and pepper. Serve the bisque hot, with a lump of crabmeat in the center, and squeeze a lime wedge over each bowl.

Wish I Was a Little Bisque Taller

Yields
3 quarts
(10 servings) The dry sherry in this recipe adds a subtle dimension to this soup, elevating it to its gourmet status (feel free to substitute brandy if that's what you have).

1 pound medium shrimp, shells on

1 tablespoon plus ½ cup unsalted butter

½ cup minced yellow onion

1 garlic clove, minced

Sea salt, to taste

Black pepper, to taste

1 tablespoon tomato paste

½ tablespoon Spanish paprika

¼ cup all-purpose flour

6 cups fish or vegetable stock

1¼ cups heavy cream

¼ teaspoon Worcestershire sauce

¼ teaspoon cayenne pepper

3 tablespoons dry sherry

1 Set a large and a medium mixing bowl in front of you. Standing over the large bowl, peel the shrimp and drop the shells into the large bowl while placing the shrimp meat in the medium bowl. Run your paring knife down the back of the shrimp to expose the vein. Use the knife or your fingers to remove the vein, and throw it away.

2 Put your 12-quart stockpot over medium heat, and add 1 tablespoon of butter. When the butter has melted, add the peeled shrimp and cook them on both sides until they are pink and just beginning to curl. This should only take 3 to 4 minutes—please do not overcook them. Overcooked shrimp are tough and rubbery and ruin a gourmet meal. Carefully remove the cooked shrimp with your tongs, and set them aside.

3 Heat the rest of the butter in the pot, and when it's melted, add the shrimp shells. Cook them, stirring occasionally, until they are bright red, about 10 minutes. Add the onions and cook for another 5 minutes, and then add the garlic to cook for 1 minute. Season them lightly with salt and pepper.

4 Continuously stirring, add the tomato paste and paprika and cook for 2 minutes.

How to Make a Foolproof Roux

A roux is a mixture of flour and fat (in this case butter) that is cooked slowly over low heat and is used to thicken mixtures such as soups and sauces. The trick to making a roux successfully is to measure carefully (there is science going on here after all) and stir it rigorously. All the flour must be incorporated into the fat or it will not only be lumpy but it may also separate later on.

Add the flour to make a roux, and cook for about 6 minutes while stirring constantly.

5 Gradually add the stock, stirring vigorously or the soup will be lumpy. Once all of the stock is incorporated, bring the soup to a very low simmer, and cook for 45 minutes, occasionally skimming any foam off the top with a large spoon and then stirring gently.

6 Using your blender and strainer, puree the soup (shells and all. These will be discarded when strained from the soup in the next step), and then strain it into another pot. Put the pureed soup over low-medium heat and stir in the cream, Worcestershire, cayenne, and sherry. Season to taste with salt and pepper. Serve warm with a cooked shrimp floating in the center of each bowl and freshly cracked pepper.

Chefology

BISQUES
What separates bisques from other soups is that they're usually very simple and have a crustacean or vegetable puree base. Classically thickened with butter and flour (known as a roux) and finished with cream, they can also employ rice, potato, or even cornstarch for thickening.

Not-for-Chickens Chicken Soup

Yields 1½ quarts (8 servings)

My good friend Maria makes a wonderful tomatillo and chipotle sauce in which she simmers chicken. Far too spicy for the likes of me, I decided to mellow it by turning the sauce into a soup, and this soup has become the most requested one in my repertoire. Using precooked chicken turns it into a one-pot wonder!

3 tablespoons vegetable oil

2 cups large diced red onion

4 carrots, large dice

1 green bell pepper, large dice

1 red bell pepper, large dice

3 garlic cloves, chopped

Sea salt, to taste

Black pepper, to taste

15 ounces diced tomato, canned

1 cup Latin Salsa Verde (p. 218)

4 to 6 chipotle peppers, canned in adobo sauce (medium to very hot) and finely chopped

3 tablespoons adobo sauce from can

8 cups vegetable stock

3 tablespoons cornstarch

1 whole roasted chicken, shredded

8 pieces corn bread (about 2-inch squares)

1 Place a 12-quart stockpot over medium to high heat and add the vegetable oil. When it begins to smoke, add the red onion, stirring until it begins to soften. Add the carrots, bell peppers, and garlic, season lightly with salt and pepper, and stir to combine. Then cover to sweat the vegetables for 5 minutes. Remove the lid, making sure all the water drains back into the pot, and sauté the vegetables 10 minutes, stirring often.

2 Carefully pour in the diced tomato, salsa verde, and finely chopped chipotle peppers, and stir to mix well. Stir constantly to keep it from scorching, and allow it to cook for 5 minutes. Add the adobo sauce and all but ¼ cup of the vegetable stock.

3 Stir the cornstarch into the ¼ cup of cold vegetable stock, making a slurry. Pour the slurry into the rest of the soup and allow it to come to a simmer. Stir occasionally as it simmers and thickens for about 20 minutes.

4 Stir in the shredded chicken and season to taste with salt and black pepper. Eat warm with fresh corn bread served family style.

Avant-Garde Avocado

Yields 1½ quarts (5 servings)

Some people erroneously assume avocados are bad for you and high in fat. Not true. The avocado only contains 4 grams of saturated fat per serving and provides lycopene, beta-carotene, and lutein to help prevent heart disease, eye disease, and some cancers. Not too crappy!

2 tablespoons extra virgin olive oil

1 yellow onion, chopped

1 garlic clove, smashed

Sea salt, to taste

Black pepper, to taste

4 ripe avocados, cubed

⅓ cup fresh squeezed lime juice

4 cups vegetable stock

2 roasted red peppers, sliced (see page 30)

1 In your 12-quart stockpot heat the olive oil over medium heat, and add the onion and garlic clove. Season lightly with salt and pepper. Cover and turn the heat to low, sweating the onions and garlic for 5 minutes. Remove the lid, but make sure the liquid that has collected in the lid falls back into the pot.

2 Leave the burner on low heat, and add the cubed avocado and lime juice. Stir until the avocado begins to break down and is completely covered by the lime juice. Add the vegetable stock, stirring constantly, until the avocado has begun to incorporate into the stock.

3 Use your blender to puree the soup in batches and pour it into another pot. Do not strain the soup. Place the pot of bisque over low heat and season to taste with salt and pepper.

4 Serve the avocado bisque warm and with a tablespoon of roasted red peppers sprinkled along the edge of the soup, or just use your leftover Pico de Gallo Salsa (p. 215).

Have-Some-Broccoli-with-That-Cheese-Soup

Yields 1 gallon (12 servings) I chose the cheeses in this recipe for their defining characteristics: cheddar for its sharpness, fontina for its nuttiness and strong aroma, Brie for both its buttery and pungent flavor, and Parmigiano for its sharp, nutty, and salty personality.

¼ cup unsalted butter

1 cup small dice yellow onion

½ cup small dice carrots

½ cup small dice celery

Sea salt, to taste

Black pepper, to taste

¼ cup all-purpose flour

4 cups chicken stock

4 cups whole milk

2 pounds broccoli florets, fresh

1 pound sharp cheddar cheese, shredded

1 pound fontina cheese, shredded

½ pound Brie cheese, rind cut off

Tabasco sauce, to taste

½ pound Parmigiano-Reggiano cheese, grated

1   In a 12-quart stockpot, heat the butter over medium heat. When the butter has completely melted, add the onion, carrot, and celery, and stir to coat with the butter. Season lightly with salt and pepper. Cover, and allow the vegetables to sweat for 5 minutes. Remove the lid, and make sure the liquid that has collected in the lid goes back into the pot.

2   While stirring constantly, add the flour to create a roux. Slowly add the chicken stock while whisking vigorously, or you will have a

Swap It

MY FRIEND JAY always wants shredded chicken in this soup. I think it's better without it, so my recipe does not include it. If you are like Jay, simply add the shredded meat of one rotisserie or roasted chicken at the very end.

lumpy soup. Once all of the stock is in, you can whisk in the milk and bring the soup up to a simmer.

3 Once simmering, add the broccoli and the cheddar, and stir until the cheddar has completely melted. Next, add the fontina and Brie, and stir until they have melted.

4 Taste the soup at this point and season it to taste with Tabasco, salt, and pepper. Serve warm with a sprinkle of Parmigiano over each bowl.

Chefology

CHEESE
With hundreds of varieties, textures, colors, and flavors, the cooking possibilities with cheese are endless. Cheese compliments wine, vegetables, most proteins, and even the most discriminating child lights up at the notion of cheese. The Crappy Little Kitchen mascot, cheese can sit in your fridge for days, and when the mold forms, you just shave that crap off and eat the rest!

Smokin' Leftover Turkey Soup

Yields
1 gallon
(12 servings)

Thanksgiving leftovers never tasted so good (and that's saying a lot!).
If you have leftover stuffing in addition to the turkey, toast it into croutons
instead of the sourdough. The family is going to think you're a genius.

½ cup unsalted butter

½ cup roughly chopped
green onion

½ cup small diced
carrots

½ cup small dice celery

Sea salt, to taste

Black pepper, to taste

¼ cup all-purpose flour

4 cups chicken stock

4 cups whole milk

1 garlic clove, minced

3 tablespoons melted
butter

1 cup cubed sourdough
bread

1 pound smoked Gouda,
shredded

1 pound smoked
cheddar, shredded

½ pound Brie, rind
cut off

4 cups shredded
roasted turkey,
white and dark meat

¼ cup chopped chives

1 Preheat oven to 400°. In a 12-quart stock-pot, heat the ½ cup of butter over medium heat. When the butter has completely melted, add the onion, carrot, and celery and stir to coat. Season lightly with salt and pepper. Sweat the vegetables gently for 10 minutes, or until the onions are translucent.

2 While stirring constantly, add the flour to create a roux. Cook the roux for 5 minutes. Slowly add the chicken stock while whisking vigorously, or you will have a lumpy soup. Once all of the stock is in, you can whisk in the milk and bring the soup up to a simmer.

3 Stir together the minced garlic and 3 tablespoons melted butter in a large mixing bowl. Toss the cubes of bread with garlic butter and put them on a baking sheet to toast in the oven for 8 to 10 minutes or until golden brown.

4 Once the soup is simmering, add the Gouda, cheddar, and Brie, and stir until the cheese has completely melted, then incorporate the shredded turkey.

5 Season to taste with salt and pepper. Serve warm with a few croutons in the center of each bowl and garnish with chopped chives.

Grilled Cheese Sandwich Soup

Yields 2½ quarts (8 servings)

This is my whimsical version of a grilled cheese sandwich with sliced tomato. It also contains my favorite elements of Welsh rarebit: a great English appetizer comprised of melted cheese sauce poured over toasted bread usually paired with crabmeat and apples. If you're feeling cheeky, garnish this with diced apple instead of tomato.

¼ cup unsalted butter

½ cup medium dice yellow onion

½ cup diced cremini mushrooms

2 garlic cloves, minced

2 teaspoons dry mustard

Sea salt, to taste

Black pepper, to taste

¼ cup all-purpose flour

5 cups chicken stock

2 cups beer (preferably a lager)

½ cup heavy cream

2 pounds sharp cheddar cheese

2 teaspoons Worcestershire sauce

Cayenne pepper, to taste

2 Roma tomatoes, small dice

1 In your 12-quart stockpot, heat the butter over medium heat. When the butter has completely melted, add the onion, mushrooms, garlic, and dry mustard. Stir to coat the vegetables with the butter and bloom (that's chef-talk for hydrate) the mustard. Season lightly with salt and pepper. Cover and allow the vegetables to sweat for 5 minutes. Remove the lid, and make sure the liquid that has collected in the lid goes back into the pot.

2 While stirring constantly, add the flour to create a roux. Slowly incorporate the chicken stock while whisking vigorously, or you will have a lumpy soup. Once all of the stock is in, you can whisk in the beer and heavy cream, and bring the soup up to a simmer. Add the cheddar cheese and Worcestershire sauce to the simmering soup, and stir until all the cheese is melted.

3 Taste the soup at this point and season to taste with cayenne, salt, and pepper. Serve this soup warm with diced tomato sprinkled on top of each bowl.

Miso Feelin' Better

Yields
2 quarts
(6 servings)

A staple in Japanese cooking, miso contains a healthy dose of isoflavones, a family of proteins known to prevent heart disease, breast cancer, and osteoporosis. To gain the most benefit from the healing properties of this recipe, do not bring the soup above a simmer once the miso is added or you will kill all the protective enzymes and deplete the flavor the miso provides. This soup garnishes itself.

6 cups vegetable stock

⅓ cup uncooked spaghetti, broken into 1-inch pieces

2 chicken breast fillets, large dice

½ cup roughly chopped green onions

½ cup fresh shitake mushrooms, no stems

½ cup chopped Napa cabbage

4 tablespoons white miso paste

Sea salt, to taste

Black pepper, to taste

1 In your 12-quart stockpot, heat the vegetable stock over high heat. Once the stock has begun to simmer, turn the heat down to medium-high and add the spaghetti. Allow the noodles to cook for 10 minutes and add the chicken.

2 When the chicken has cooked through, which should only take about 5 minutes, add the onions, mushrooms, and cabbage. Turn the heat down to medium and add the miso one tablespoon at a time, until all the paste dissolves, being careful to keep the soup below a boil.

3 Taste the soup at this point to see if it needs any salt or pepper. Miso pastes vary in salty flavor, so always taste before adding any salt. Serve warm and right away.

Not-So-Basic Black Bean Soup

Yields
1 gallon
(12 servings)

You can make this in a jiffy by using a 30-ounce can of black beans, and beginning with step two. Super CLK friendly!

2 cups dried black beans

½ cup small-diced smoked bacon

1 yellow onion, small dice

2 celery stalks, small dice

1 green bell pepper, small dice

2 garlic cloves, minced

Sea salt, to taste

Black pepper, to taste

8 cups vegetable stock

2 bay leaves

3 tablespoons chopped fresh thyme leaves

3 tablespoons chopped fresh oregano leaves

½ teaspoon lemon zest

¼ cup chopped Italian parsley

¼ cup dry sherry

2 lemons, sliced extremely thin (3 slices per bowl of soup)

1 Sort through your black beans, and pick out any rocks or malformed beans. In a 12-quart stockpot, soak the beans in 4 quarts of water overnight. Rinse the beans well the next day in your steamer basket. While they're draining, dry the stockpot.

2 Put the pot over medium to high heat, and add the diced bacon. Allow the fat to render (or melt out of the bacon) for about 10 minutes, stirring often. Add the vegetables and turn the heat down to medium. Season lightly with salt and pepper, and cover the pot to allow the vegetables to sweat for 10 minutes. When you remove the lid, be sure all the liquid that has collected goes back into the pot.

3 Pour the beans back into the stockpot and stir together with the vegetables. Add the vegetable stock and bay leaves; cover, reduce the heat to low, and allow the soup to cook slowly for 1 hour.

4 Puree half of the bean mixture in your blender. Add the pureed black beans back into the pot with the fresh thyme, oregano, lemon zest, parsley, and sherry. Season to taste with salt or pepper.

5 Serve warm with 3 slices of lemon floating on the soup's surface to garnish the center of each bowl.

Vichyssoise
by No Other Name

**Yields
1 gallon
(12 servings)**

Despite its restaurant workhorse title, vichyssoise (vee-shee-so-AHZ) is the quintessential gourmet soup, and it's easy to make at home in your CLK. To keep the soup free of floating flecks of herbs but to infuse it with flavor, chefs make an herb and spice "sachet" using a square of cheesecloth tied with butcher's twine. I use a sock, which is perfect CLK ingenuity. My dad taught me this trick in high school when we competed together in my first chili competition.

4 tablespoons unsalted butter

6 leeks, finely chopped, washed and dried

1 yellow onion, finely chopped

Sea salt, to taste

4 parsley stems

1 whole clove

½ teaspoon whole black peppercorns

1 bay leaf

Brand new, thin white sock (I'm not kidding!)

1 pound sweet potatoes, peeled and diced

½ pound russet potatoes, peeled and diced

6 cups chicken stock

3 cups half and half

White pepper, to taste

¼ teaspoon nutmeg

3 teaspoons chopped chives

1 In a 12-quart stockpot, heat the butter over medium heat. When all the butter has melted, add the leeks and onions, season them lightly with salt, and sweat them until they are tender and translucent. During this time, put the parsley, clove, black pepper, and bay leaf into the white sock, and tie the top very tightly. This is the perfect CLK sachet.

2 Add the potatoes, chicken stock, and sachet to the pot and raise the temperature to high, bringing the soup to a full boil. Now reduce the heat to medium, cover and simmer until the potatoes start to fall apart, about 20 to 25 minutes. Remove the sachet and throw it away (unless you want to dump out the herbs and try washing the sock for future wear).

3 Using your blender, puree all of the soup and place it in the refrigerator to chill. Once completely cool, whisk in the half and half, taste the soup, and season to taste with sea salt, white pepper, and nutmeg. Serve ice-cold, and sprinkle a pinch of chive in the center of each bowl.

Cure All with Curry

Yields
2 quarts
(6 servings)

Curry is a blend of spices that generally includes turmeric, coriander, and cumin—all of which have valuable healing properties. Turmeric not only provides yellow color but also helps to fight cancer. Coriander, aids with digestion, acts as a natural diuretic, and helps the body detoxify. Cumin stimulates circulation and can help relieve abdominal cramping. So long story short, eat more curry, and you won't feel so crappy!

3 tablespoons extra virgin olive oil

3 cups small dice yellow onion

1 tablespoon minced garlic

1 tablespoon minced fresh ginger

Sea salt, to taste

Black pepper, to taste

2 tablespoons curry powder (yellow)

2 tablespoons red curry paste

½ tablespoon Hungarian paprika

1 cup white wine

32 ounces diced tomato, canned

4 cups vegetable stock

¼ cup crème fraiche, or sour cream

1 In a 12-quart stockpot, heat the olive oil over medium heat. Add the onion, garlic, and ginger, and allow them to sweat slowly. You want them to soften, not brown. Season lightly with salt and pepper.

2 When the onions are translucent, add the curry powder, curry paste, and paprika, and cook for 5 to 6 minutes, stirring constantly. Add the white wine and bring the soup to a simmer. Allow the wine to reduce by half, and then add the canned tomato and vegetable stock. Turn the heat down slightly and allow the soup to cook slowly for 30 minutes.

3 Remove from heat and season to taste with salt and pepper. Serve piping hot with a tablespoon of crème fraiche in the center of each bowl of soup.

Hold-the-Beef Minestrone

Yields 1½ quarts (18 servings)

This huge recipe serves eighteen people easily, but it's so delicious you'll be happy to have the leftovers. If you don't think you'll be able to finish eating it all in a few days, follow the instructions, but leave out the pasta. Freeze the soup in several batches using freezer bags or containers. Pull a portion of the frozen soup out to leave in the fridge the day before you'd like to eat it. Bring the defrosted soup to a slow boil, add the pasta, and it will be ready to eat in 8 to 10 minutes! That's how you get gourmet minestrone on demand.

1 cup dried cannellini or borlotti beans

8 cups water

3 tablespoons extra virgin olive oil

1 yellow onion, medium dice

2 garlic cloves, minced

Sea salt, to taste

Black pepper, to taste

15 ounces crushed tomatoes, canned

1 teaspoon red pepper flakes

2 bay leaves

1 cup peeled and diced carrots

½ cup diced celery

1 russet potato, peeled and diced (about 1½ cups)

4 cups shredded green kale

20 cups (5 quarts) vegetable stock

1½ cups diced zucchini squash

¼ cups uncooked ditalini pasta or small macaroni

½ cup chopped basil

½ cup finely grated Parmesan-Reggiano

1 Sort through your beans, and pick out any rocks or malformed beans. In a 12-quart stockpot, soak the beans in 8 cups of water overnight. Rinse the beans well the next day, and while they're draining, dry the stockpot.

2 Put the pot over medium heat, and add the olive oil, onion, and garlic. Season lightly with salt and pepper. Cook slowly so the heat pulls out their natural

Swap It

YOU CAN SUBSTITUTE a 30-ounce can of cannellini beans for the dried. Use them rinsed straight from the can, and start at step two.

Crappy Little Kitchens

moisture and the onion becomes translucent, about 8 minutes. Add the entire can of crushed tomatoes, the red pepper flakes, and bay leaves into the pot, and allow them to come to a boil without raising the temperature. Add the diced carrots, celery, and potato, and cook for 5 minutes, stirring constantly. Season lightly with sea salt; this helps your tomatoes break down while seasoning all the vegetables. Stir in the shredded kale, and cook for 5 minutes.

3 Add vegetable stock, and raise the temperature to bring the soup to a boil. Turn the heat down to a simmer, cover, and cook the minestrone until the beans are tender, about an hour and a half.

4 Carefully drop in your zucchini and cook until softened, about 4 minutes, and then add the pasta and cook for another 8 minutes. Taste the soup at this point to see if it needs more salt, and it will certainly need freshly cracked black pepper. Let the soup cool slightly for 5 minutes to allow the flavors to blend, and garnish each bowl with a pinch of fresh basil and grated Parmesan.

Did You Know This Crap?

The popular white beans known as cannellini are actually beige in color and have a traditional kidney shape. With a slightly nutty taste and mild earthiness, they have a relatively thin skin and tender, creamy flesh. For unexpected variety, look for borlotti beans, also known as cranberry beans or French horticultural beans. These beautiful beans have colorful red markings, and nutty flavor and a creamy texture similar to the cannellini. Although popular in Italian and Portuguese cuisine, most borlotti beans sold in Italy are cranberry beans imported from the United States.

Toss Everything but These Salads

For a Good Time Call . . .
Champagne Oysters, p. 46

Scallops Ceviche, p. 48

Bloody Mary Bloody Mary
Blood Mary Relish, p. 41

Miso Feelin' Better Soup, p. 68

Gazpacho Margarita, Ole! p. 58

Avant Garde Avocado Soup, p. 63

Fresh-Faced Asparagus Salad, p. 92

My Big Fat Greek Salad, p. 79

Heirloom Tomato Stack, p. 81

Whats-a-Matta-You Bruschetta Salad, p. 88

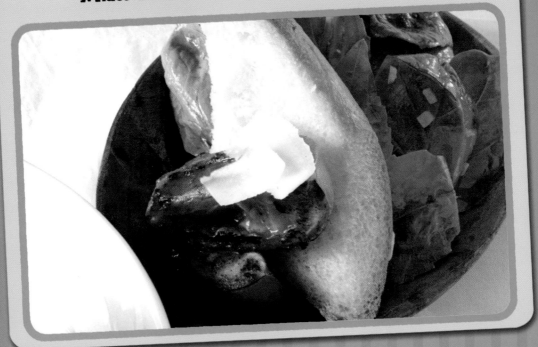

Salads by nature are CLK friendly because, for the most part, all the ingredients get tossed in one bowl. Not so long ago, boring iceberg lettuce graced the tables of fine restaurants and homes alike, thanks to its crisp texture and long shelf life. In recent years, the gourmet world and the at-home cook have embraced a variety of tasty leaf options—from arugula and romaine to endive and watercress—they add taste, texture, nutrition, and color to the ho-hum salads of yesteryear. To me, iceberg tastes like nothing more than pale green water. If you want a light and simple salad, go bright green. The more color, the more nutrients and flavor, because a healthy Crappy Little Kitchen is a happy Crappy Little Kitchen.

Salads create limitless possibilities, so mix and match your greens and vegetables with what you have on hand or what looks the freshest at your grocery store.

The King of Caesar Salads

Serves 8

Every gourmet chef needs a good Caesar salad recipe in her repertoire and this one is great! Add some grilled chicken, beef, or fish on top to make this dish a satisfying meal.

2 egg yolks

2 garlic cloves

3 anchovies

1 teaspoon Dijon mustard

¼ cup lemon juice

3 tablespoons balsamic vinegar

1½ cups extra virgin olive oil

¼ cup shredded Pecorino Romano cheese

Sea salt, to taste

Black pepper, to taste

2 heads romaine lettuce, roughly chopped

¼ cup shaved Parmigiano-Reggiano

1 Pulse the egg yolks, garlic, anchovies, and mustard in your blender until well combined. Add the lemon juice and balsamic vinegar and pulse to combine. Drizzle in the olive oil while blending at medium speed to emulsify the dressing. It should become thick and creamy. Gently pulse in the shredded cheese; don't overpuree it or it will get thick and gummy. Taste the dressing at this point and season to taste with salt and pepper.

2 Put the chopped lettuce in a large bowl and toss with about ½ cup of the dressing. Taste a piece of lettuce to see if it is well dressed. If it's too dry, add more dressing. Garnish with the shaved Parmesan cheese. To make individual portions, pile the salad high in bowls, and garnish with shaved Parmesan. For that gourmet boost, top each salad with half a soft-boiled egg.

Store any leftover dressing in an airtight container in the refrigerator, and it's ready for next time. Leftover Caesar dressing is great for dipping French fries. I'm not kidding. Try it!

My Big Fat Greek Salad

The colorful fresh veggies in this recipe make the presentation beautiful on its own, and its mixture of flavors and textures makes it impressive for the most discerning guests.

1 tablespoon Dijon mustard

1 teaspoon minced anchovy (1 or 2)

¼ cup fresh oregano

¼ cup sherry vinegar

1 cup extra virgin olive oil

Sea salt, to taste

Black pepper, to taste

¼ cup diced English cucumber

2 Roma tomatoes, diced

¼ cup diced red onion

¼ cup chopped kalamata olives

3 tablespoons crumbled feta cheese, plus extra for garnish

1 cup thinly sliced romaine lettuce (use your bread knife to make thin slices from a head of romaine)

4 slices sourdough bread, toasted

1 In your blender, pulse the mustard, anchovy, and oregano until mixed. Add the sherry vinegar and pulse until well combined. While blending at medium speed, drizzle in the olive oil and season to taste with salt and pepper.

2 In a large bowl, toss the cucumber, tomato, onion, olives, feta cheese, and romaine with ½ cup of the dressing. Taste the salad to see if it needs more dressing, salt, or pepper.

3 Mound the salad in a large serving bowl. Cut the toasted bread into wedges, tuck the wedges around, and garnish it with more crumbled feta. For individual portions, hold the toasted bread wedge in the center of each small plate, and pile the salad high around it. This makes each plate look like a sailboat. You could also serve individual salad portions in margarita or martini glasses with the toast jutting out like a sail.

4 Store the leftover dressing in an airtight container in the refrigerator. You can toss the leftover salad as well as the dressing with some pasta for a great Greek pasta salad.

This Salad Bites

Serves 8 to 10

Fresh arugula is extra spicy and peppery, which is perfect for this lemon vinaigrette. Buying baby greens like baby arugula and baby spinach means no chopping and no washing, so they scream CLK friendly!

1 shallot, chopped

2 lemons, zested and juiced

1 tablespoon ground coriander

¼ cup rice wine vinegar

1 cup extra virgin olive oil

Sea salt, to taste

Black pepper, to taste

1 pound baby spinach

1 pound baby arugula

½ cup pine nuts, toasted

¼ cup French goat cheese

1 In your blender, pulse the shallot, lemon zest, and coriander until combined. While on a low speed, drizzle in the lemon juice and rice wine vinegar. Increase the speed to medium and slowly drizzle in the olive oil. Season to taste with salt and pepper.

2 Put the spinach and arugula in a large bowl and toss with about ¼ cup of the dressing. Taste to see if the dressing needs more salt or pepper. Garnish with the pine nuts and crumbles of goat cheese. Plate individual portions exactly the same way. For that extra gourmet touch, add thinly sliced pears in the shape of a fan beneath the goat cheese and pine nuts.

3 Store any leftover dressing in an airtight container in the refrigerator, and use it as a wonderful chicken marinade.

Heirloom Tomato Stack

Serves 4

This recipe comes together with no cooking or tossing of any kind. You can make this salad from cutting board to plate in 30 seconds flat with no dirty dishes.

4 heirloom tomatoes, various colors

Sea salt, to taste

Black pepper, to taste

¼ cup aged (at least 6 months) balsamic vinegar

3 tablespoons chopped Italian parsley

1 Slice the tomatoes into one-fourth-inch thick disks, which should be about four slices from each tomato. Liberally salt and pepper each tomato slice. In the center of each salad plate, stack the tomatoes slightly askew alternating colors four tomatoes high.

2 Drizzle the balsamic vinegar over and around the outside of the stacks on the plate and garnish the top slice with the chopped parsley. Serve the salads at room temperature, and enjoy the epitome of the gourmet "no-pot" wonder!

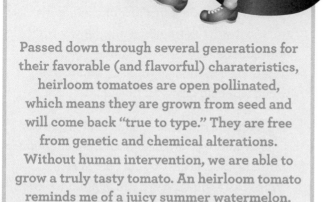

Did You Know This Crap?

Passed down through several generations for their favorable (and flavorful) charateristics, heirloom tomatoes are open pollinated, which means they are grown from seed and will come back "true to type." They are free from genetic and chemical alterations. Without human intervention, we are able to grow a truly tasty tomato. An heirloom tomato reminds me of a juicy summer watermelon, and it's unnecessary to enhance its flavor with anything more than salt and pepper.

Bacon-Boosted
Red Cabbage Salad

Serves 15

The applewood-smoked bacon in this recipe provides a layer of depth to the sweet and sour braised cabbage that elevates this dish to gourmet status. Chefs agree that many recipes can benefit from the addition of bacon, and this recipe is no exception.

2 tablespoons olive oil

½ cup medium diced applewood smoked bacon

1 red onion, thinly sliced

Sea salt, to taste

1 small head red cabbage, thinly sliced into shreds

Black pepper, to taste

¾ cup red wine vinegar

½ cup sugar

4 ounces Roquefort blue cheese, crumbled

1 Preheat a 12-inch sauté pan on medium heat. When it is hot, carefully add the olive oil and bacon. The bacon should begin to cook slightly and render its fat and flavor into the oil, so only cook it for about 3 minutes. Don't allow it to overcrisp since it will continue cooking when the other ingredients are added. Add the red onion and sauté lightly for another 3 minutes, moving the onions around constantly to keep them from browning. We just want to draw out their natural liquid, and seasoning them with a little salt will help them along.

2 When the onions are translucent and the bacon is crispy, carefully add the cabbage, and feel free to do it in shifts one handful at a time so it wilts down efficiently. Slowly cook down the cabbage. As the cabbage begins to soften, season to taste with salt and pepper, which will help draw out the liquid.

3 Add the red wine vinegar and sugar, and allow the entire dish to simmer and reduce until the juice at the bottom becomes thick syrup. Taste the cabbage at this point to see if any more salt or pepper is needed.

4 Serve this salad warm with the blue cheese crumbled over the top, allowing it to melt slightly from the heat of the cabbage. For individual portions, pile the cabbage high in the center of the salad plate and garnish with the Roquefort. You can also sprinkle the salad with toasted walnut pieces (place them on a baking sheet and into a 350° oven for about 10 minutes) to add crunch to the salad.

Swap It

FEEL FREE to experiment with different flavors of smoked bacon for this recipe. Gourmet markets offer a wide assortment including cinnamon and green tea smoked—choose your favorite and invoke unique personality and flavor into this salad. Whatever you do, don't use just any crappy bacon, because this ingredient is integral to the final outcome of the dish.

Poblano Slaw

Serves 10

A vibrant, crisp salad with a bit of a kick, no one will believe this Latin-fusion slaw, which is a far cry from your grandmother's soggy stuff, came out of your Crappy Little Kitchen.

3 poblano peppers

3 tablespoons extra virgin olive oil

1 cup kosher salt

½ head red cabbage, shredded

½ head green cabbage, shredded

4 limes, juiced

¼ cup rice wine vinegar

1 tablespoon sugar

1 teaspoon ground cumin

¼ cup real mayonnaise

4 green onions, chopped (both green and white part)

1 carrot, peeled and grated

Sea salt, to taste

Black pepper, to taste

1 Preheat your oven to 500°. Place the poblano peppers on your baking sheet and drizzle olive oil over them. Roast them in the oven for 15 to 20 minutes or until they begin to blacken and blister all over. Remove them with your tongs, and place them in a mixing bowl and cover with plastic wrap. Allow them to sit this way and steam.

2 While you are waiting for them to cool, generously salt (we will rinse it off, so be sure to use enough salt to coat all of the cabbage) both cabbages using one cup kosher salt (kosher salt has a fairly large grain and will not dissolve before completing its duty of drawing out the liquid inside the cabbage), and allow them to drain in your steamer basket for an hour. Rinse thoroughly with cool water, shake to remove as much water as possible, and drain for about another 10 minutes.

3 Once the peppers are cool, pull off their tops and dump out the seeds and juice. Carefully peel off their skins, but don't rinse under water or you'll lose too much flavor! Cut them in a medium dice.

How to Shred Cabbage by Hand

Use your chef's knife to cut the head of cabbage through the core into four wedges. Cut the core out of each wedge. Place a wedge, with a cut side down, on a cutting board. Hold your chef's knife perpendicular to the cabbage and slice it into long thin strips.

4 In a large bowl, combine the lime juice, vinegar, sugar, cumin, and mayonnaise. Add the cabbage, roasted poblano, green onion, and carrot and toss. Taste at this point and season as needed with salt and pepper. Chill it for at least an hour, and serve ice cold. Simply pile the slaw high in the center of a platter for a colorful presentation. I feel the only way to serve this is family style, unless you're using it to garnish fish tacos!

Cherry Tomatoes with Tamarind Glaze

Serves 6

Watch this beautiful salad come together in eight minutes with the use of only one small sauté pan. Majorly CLK-friendly. The glaze is a showstopper on wild birds as well.

½ teaspoon cumin seeds

½ teaspoon fennel seeds

2 teaspoons tamarind concentrate

2 tablespoons hot water

2 teaspoons honey

2 tablespoons extra virgin olive oil

Sea salt, to taste

Black pepper, to taste

1 pint red cherry tomatoes, halved

1 pint green cherry tomatoes, halved

1 pint yellow cherry tomatoes, halved

1 bunch cilantro leaves, ¼ cup chopped, plus more for garnish

1 Heat up your 8-inch nonstick sauté pan over medium heat, and add the cumin and fennel seeds. Toast them until they begin to smell aromatic, and then chop them roughly on your cutting board once cooled.

2 In a medium bowl, add the tamarind, hot water, and honey, and whisk in the toasted cumin and fennel. While whisking, drizzle in the olive oil to create a glaze, and season to your taste with salt and pepper.

Swap It

THERE ARE MANY varieties of small tomatoes. Here I like to use cherry tomatoes because they're small while being large enough to cut in half. If they're not available, pear or currant tomatoes can be substituted, just leave them whole. In a pinch, simply use all red cherry tomatoes or large dice some plum tomatoes, which come in red, yellow, and green varieties.

3 Toss the tomatoes and ¼ cup chopped cilantro leaves with the glaze, and taste to see if you need more salt or pepper. Serve at room temperature, piled high on individual salad plates, with a few cilantro leaves on top.

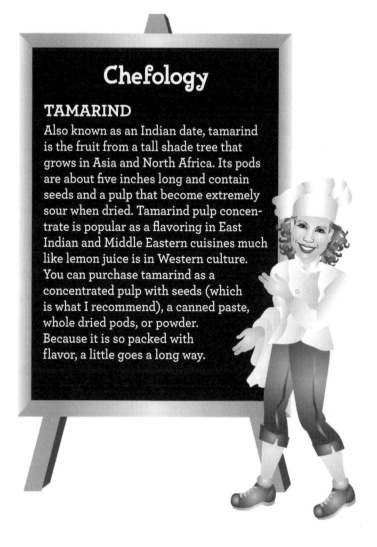

Chefology

TAMARIND

Also known as an Indian date, tamarind is the fruit from a tall shade tree that grows in Asia and North Africa. Its pods are about five inches long and contain seeds and a pulp that become extremely sour when dried. Tamarind pulp concentrate is popular as a flavoring in East Indian and Middle Eastern cuisines much like lemon juice is in Western culture. You can purchase tamarind as a concentrated pulp with seeds (which is what I recommend), a canned paste, whole dried pods, or powder. Because it is so packed with flavor, a little goes a long way.

Whats-a-Matta-You Bruschetta Salad

Serves 6

We are all familiar with traditional bruschetta as an appetizer, but I just love the idea of a deconstructed bruschetta becoming a salad. All the elements are here: toasted bread, tomato, basil, and cheese. Not intended for a large platter presentation, this salad "plates up" on individual salad plates in minutes with very little clean up.

3 Roma tomatoes

1 French baguette

¼ cup extra virgin olive oil

Sea salt, to taste

Black pepper, to taste

2 garlic cloves

2 tablespoons minced shallot

2 tablespoons sherry wine vinegar

1 teaspoon Dijon mustard

1 bunch basil leaves

⅓ cup extra virgin olive oil

Sea salt, to taste

Black pepper, to taste

8 ounces fresh baby spinach

¼ cup shaved Parmigiano-Reggiano

1 Preheat your oven to 400°. Cut the tomatoes in half lengthwise, then again making 4 wedges per tomato, and place them skin down on a baking sheet. Using your bread knife, cut the baguette into 3-inch segments, and then cut the segments in half, lengthwise. Put 6 of the pieces of bread on the baking sheet, crust down, next to the tomatoes.

2 Drizzle the tomatoes and bread with olive oil and season the tomatoes liberally (tomatoes have a lot of water and require a good amount of salt to taste their best) with salt and pepper, with just a light touch of salt on the bread. Put the tray in the oven for 20 minutes until the bread is toasted, and the tomatoes have begun to brown. Rub the raw garlic cloves on the toasted bread.

3 In your blender, add the shallot, sherry wine vinegar, Dijon mustard, and 8 basil leaves. Pulse until well combined. Put the blender on low speed, and drizzle in ⅓ cup of olive oil. Season to your taste with salt and pepper.

4 Remove the stems from the rest of the basil. In a large bowl, toss the basil and spinach with half of the dressing. Taste a piece of the spinach to see if it needs more dressing, salt, or pepper. On six chilled plates, mound one handful of the dressed greens, place a toasted piece of baguette on top, and crown the baguette with two roasted tomatoes. Garnish the tomatoes with shaved Parmesan, and serve immediately.

Chefology

DECONSTRUCTED DISH

Taking the parts of a dish or recipe and separating the individual components into a new usage. The pieces should be recognizable by themselves but when eaten together should bring about the idea of the original dish. Think in terms of the whole is the sum of its parts.

Haricot Vert Almondine

Serves 4

Make this tasty green bean salad a day in advance and serve it on a hot summer day. The crisp bright beans will never wilt or lose their visual appeal, even after an hour of waiting on your crappy little counter for late guests to arrive.

1 pound French green beans, tops removed

Sea salt, as needed

¼ cup rice wine vinegar

2 teaspoons soy sauce

1 tablespoon minced garlic

2 teaspoons minced fresh ginger

2 teaspoons honey

1 pinch red pepper flakes

½ teaspoon sesame oil

¾ cup extra virgin olive oil

¼ cup sliced almonds, toasted

1 Blanch (p. 91) the beans for one minute then shock them.

2 In a medium mixing bowl, whisk together the vinegar, soy sauce, garlic, ginger, honey, pepper flakes, and sesame oil. Once

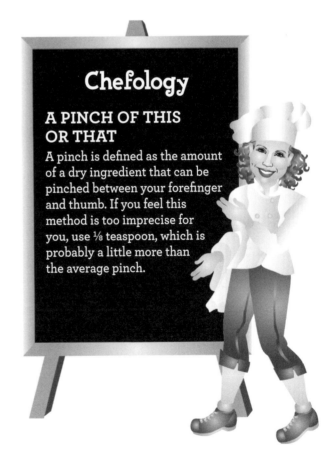

Chefology

A PINCH OF THIS OR THAT

A pinch is defined as the amount of a dry ingredient that can be pinched between your forefinger and thumb. If you feel this method is too imprecise for you, use ⅛ teaspoon, which is probably a little more than the average pinch.

Crappy Little Kitchens

Blanching and Shocking

Blanching and shocking involve briefly boiling vegetables and then quickly stopping the cooking process by immediately submerging them in an ice bath. This will not only heighten color but also remove bitter flavors. Fill your 12-quart stockpot halfway with water and place it over high heat. While your pot of water is coming to a boil, fill a large bowl halfway up with ice and water to create an ice bath for your veggies. Before your water boils, at the point when bubbles begin to form at the bottom of the pot, add a pinch of salt. If it sinks to the bottom, your water isn't hot enough, so wait a few minutes and try again. If a cloud forms as the salt is dissolved, your water is ready. Now you may continue adding salt, a little at a time, until the cloud no longer forms and the salt settles at the bottom. This means that your water is "supersaturated" and perfectly salted for blanching.

When the water reaches a rolling boil, carefully drop in one handful of vegetables. Allow them to boil (anywhere from 45 seconds to 2 minutes, depending on the vegetable) and then use your tongs or spider to remove the veggies from the water and drop them into the bowl of ice water until they have cooled. Then dry them on paper towel or a clean dish towel. Wait for the stockpot to again reach a rolling boil and add another handful of vegetables and repeat the process until all your vegetables are cooked and chilled.

• •

well combined, slowly whisk in the olive oil.

3 Toss the chilled green beans with ¼ cup of the dressing, and taste a bean at this point to see if it needs more dressing or any salt. Store any extra dressing in an airtight container and refrigerate.

4 Divide the green beans evenly amongst four salad plates, and garnish with the toasted almonds. Drizzle some extra dressing around the outside of the plate.

Fresh-Faced Asparagus Salad

Serves 4

The tangy, creamy dressing that graces this asparagus salad trumps the traditional hollandaise sauce with no fuss, and a vibrant presentation. It whisks together in one bowl, making it very CLK friendly.

1 pound asparagus, tough ends trimmed off (break one end off to see about where the asparagus would naturally separate and then trim the rest to the same length)

Sea salt, as needed

2 tablespoons raspberry vinegar

1 teaspoon Dijon mustard

4 tablespoons crème fraiche or sour cream

1 pinch ground white pepper

1 cup fresh raspberries

1 Blanch the asparagus for two minutes, and then shock it.

2 In a small bowl, whisk together the raspberry vinegar, mustard, crème fraiche, and white pepper. Season to taste with salt.

3 Divide the asparagus evenly among four salad plates with all the asparagus tips facing the same way, but piled high on top of each other. Drizzle the dressing through the middle of each pile of asparagus, and garnish the plates with the fresh raspberries dropped strategically around the plate. To present on a platter, pile the asparagus high in a long and jagged "fence post" fashion and drizzle the dressing around the outside of the platter in an attractive pattern. Garnish sporadically with fresh raspberries.

Presto!
Pesto Potato Salad

Serves 8

Try this innovative version of the traditional potato salad you grew up eating. The bright colors and varied textures ramp up the gourmet factor and make garnishing unnecessary.

5 red potatoes (about 2 pounds)

Sea salt, to taste

8 sun dried tomatoes, chopped

¼ cup chopped fresh basil

4 tablespoons toasted and chopped pine nuts

¼ cup mayonnaise

¼ cup basil pesto (see p. 220)

Black pepper, to taste

1 Fill your 12-quart stockpot with the potatoes, and cover them with water. Put the pot over high heat, and wait for it to begin to simmer. When the water has begun to bubble, add 2 tablespoons of sea salt to the water and allow the potatoes to simmer until just tender, about 15–20 minutes. Don't boil the potatoes! You want a gentle simmer in which you only see very small bubbles breaking the surface. Boiling will cause the potato skins to tear and the potato will get waterlogged. Not to mention, the outside of the potato will be soft when the inside is still raw. Drain the potatoes, put them in a large bowl, and refrigerate.

2 When the potatoes are cooled, carefully cut each potato into large cubes. Very carefully fold in the tomatoes, basil, pine nuts, mayonnaise, and pesto. You don't want to break down your potatoes too much, so be gentle! Taste the potato salad to see if you need more salt or pepper.

3 Pile high on a serving platter, and wrap tightly to refrigerate until you're ready to serve ice cold.

Swap It

SUBSTITUTE blue and white fingerling potatoes for the red potatoes, and toss with store-bought sun-dried tomato pesto for a colorful and patriotic holiday version of this potato salad!

Carmelized Fennel and Goat Cheese with Roasted Tomato Vinaigrette

Serves 4

Once the fennel is roasted, this dish is ready to plate, so your Crappy Little Kitchen will thank you. Just leave the roasted fennel in a super low oven until you're ready to serve.

3 Roma tomatoes

½ cup extra virgin olive oil, evenly divided

Sea salt, as needed

Black pepper, as needed

3 garlic cloves

4 tablespoons balsamic vinegar

4 baby fennel, halved

1 lemon, juiced

5 ounces goat cheese

1 tablespoon fresh thyme leaves

¼ cup vegetable stock

1 Preheat oven to 450°. Slice the tomatoes in half and place them skin side down on a sheet tray. Drizzle the tomatoes with ¼ cup of olive oil, and season them liberally with sea salt and pepper. Roast them in the oven for 15 minutes, turn the turn the tray, and add the garlic cloves, roasting for another 5 minutes. Leave the oven on.

Did You Know This Crap?

A member of the carrot family, fennel is an aromatic vegetable like celery and carrots, but it has a distinct anise flavor. It has a white bulb on one end with tough, green stalks growing out of it. Some people avoid fennel because of its strong licorice flavor in the raw. When cooked, fennel develops a mellow, delicate flavor. Look for white or very pale green fennel bulbs with bright green, firm stalks and fronds.

2 Pour the roasted tomatoes, garlic, and all the juices from the sheet tray into your blender, add the balsamic vinegar, and set the blender aside.

3 Place the fennel, cut side down on that same baking sheet and drizzle it with ¼ cup of olive oil and the lemon juice. Don't add any salt or pepper yet. Put it in the oven for 15 to 20 minutes or until golden brown. Place 2 slices of goat cheese on the white base of each fennel bulb, sprinkle the whole pan with the thyme leaves and salt and pepper, and return the pan to the oven. Bake until the top of the goat cheese has begun to bubble and brown.

4 Pulse the contents of the blender and slowly drizzle in the stock. Season to taste with salt and pepper.

5 Take four salad plates and place two fennel bulbs with goat cheese in the center of each. Drizzle the tomato vinaigrette in a circle around the cheese, and serve warm. It just doesn't have the same dramatic effect on a platter, so I always serve this dish on individual salad plates.

Beat This Balsamic Egg Salad

Here's a twist on traditional egg salad. Balsamic vinegar serves as the secret gourmet ingredient that elevates this salad to spectacular!

12 eggs

1 bunch scallions

¼ cup balsamic vinegar, aged at least 3 years (anything aged less than 3 years isn't really balsamic vinegar)

¼ cup real mayonnaise

3 tablespoons chopped fresh dill

Sea salt, to taste

Black pepper, to taste

2 Roma tomatoes, thinly sliced

1 Carefully place the eggs in your 12-quart stockpot, cover them with water, and put them on a burner at high heat. Bring to a rapid boil. The very second they boil, remove the pot

Did You Know This Crap?

A scallion, commonly known as green onion or spring onion, is an immature onion harvested before a prominent bulb has formed. Technically scallions should have no bulb at all, while green onions should have a small bulb. Both the white and green parts are edible. Recipes may call for using the white, green, or both parts. In most recipes, the white part is cooked and the green part is used as a garnish. In a pinch, you can substitute the green part for chives.

The Easy Peel

Once your hard-boiled egg has cooled, tap the widest end of the egg (or what would appear to be the bottom) on a flat surface. This will expose the air pocket between the egg and the shell, giving you an easy spot to start peeling. Since you won't overcook the egg (see method on p. 96) the shell should release easily.

from the heat, and cover for 10 minutes. Remove the cover and allow the eggs to cool. This is the foolproof method for making perfectly medium boiled eggs every time. You'll never have a green layer form on the outside of the yolk or have an impossible egg to peel again. I give you the CLK-friendly egg!

2 Peel the eggs and roughly chop them up into small pieces, then put the chopped eggs into a large mixing bowl. Thinly slice the white and green parts of the scallion, reserving a handful of the green parts for the garnish.

3 Add the balsamic vinegar and mayonnaise to the eggs, and fold the mixture together very gently, until just combined. Now fold in the dill and onions. Season to taste with salt and pepper.

4 Evenly cover your serving platter with the tomato slices and lightly season with salt and pepper. Top the tomato layer with egg salad, sprinkle with the reserved green parts of the scallion, wrap tightly with plastic wrap, and refrigerate for several hours. Serve ice cold.

Wassup!
Wasabi Chicken Salad

Serves 8

The Asian-style barbeque dressing imparts both a creamy and spicy flavor, while the onions and peanuts provide a lovely crunch to the pale green salad. You can substitute slivered almonds for the peanuts without crapping out on this gourmet recipe.

Sea salt, to taste

1 pound chicken breasts, boneless and skinless

1 pound chicken thighs, boneless and skinless

½ cup rice wine vinegar

2 tablespoons wasabi powder

2 tablespoons sour cream

¼ cup extra virgin olive oil

1 tablespoon soy sauce

1 tablespoon grated fresh ginger

1 clove garlic, minced

Black pepper, to taste

3 tablespoons chopped fresh mint

3 tablespoons chopped fresh cilantro

¼ cup thinly sliced red onion

¼ cup peanuts, toasted

½ cup roughly chopped dried apricots

Napa cabbage leaves, as needed

1 tablespoon black sesame seed (the black adds color contrast to the dish)

1. Fill your 12-quart stockpot halfway with water, and put on a burner at high heat. When it begins to simmer, add 3 tablespoons of sea salt and let it dissolve. Using your chef's knife, remove the fat from the chicken.

2. When the water comes to a boil, turn the heat slightly down. Use your tongs to gently set the breasts and thighs into the pot. Simmer them for exactly 10 minutes, then remove them with your tongs, and put them into a bowl and cover with ice. Allow them to chill for about 5 minutes and remove from the ice. Pat dry. Roughly chop the chicken into fairly small pieces, and toss into a mixing bowl.

3. Put the rice wine vinegar in your blender, and sprinkle the wasabi powder over it. Add the sour cream and pulse the mixture until smooth, and then slowly drizzle in the olive oil while blending on a low speed. Add the soy sauce, ginger, and garlic, then pulse to combine. Season to taste with salt and pepper.

4 Add about ¼ cup of the dressing to the chopped chicken and toss lightly to combine. Add the mint, cilantro, onion, peanuts, and apricots and toss again. Taste the salad at this point to see if you would like more dressing, salt, or pepper.

5 Cover your serving platter with Napa cabbage leaves and mound the chicken salad on top. Wrap tightly and store in the refrigerator until ready to serve. Serve ice cold and garnish with black sesame seeds.

Swap It

YOU CAN SWITCH up protein sources in your salad recipes. Make wasabi potato salad, pesto egg salad, or balsamic chicken salad. Decide what best suits your guests, your menu, the occasion, and your Crappy Little Kitchen. I envisioned these salads as picnic-style recipes, so I recommend plating them as platters, but please feel free to experiment with them on individual plates for lunch by using your favorite bread for sandwiches or topping a large dinner salad.

Exquisite
Entrées

At last, the main event! Don't let crappy service get in the way of your gourmet dining dreams. Here you will learn how to prepare complete meals at home that look and taste like they came from a five-star restaurant.

Fine dining establishments put great effort into serving food that looks superb on the plate, and in chef-talk we call this presentation. One of the easiest ways to achieve a gourmet presentation is to add height to the food on the plate. Carefully consider side dishes and accompaniments for your entrée that will literally help your dish stand up. The Snake-Charmin' Moroccan Lamb Chops can stand on their own bones to create dramatic height, which is why they can be paired with the Saffron Couscous that doesn't have much volume, while the Stuffed Chicken Breast might need a buttery mound of Garlic Whipped Potatoes to lean on.

> The Key to gourmet presentation involves arranging the food in an interesting manner and garnishing the plate to add color and contrast.

Color plays an imperative role in successful presentation. Garnish and choose side dishes that will compliment the main entrée. Each element on the plate should "pop" with color as well as flavor. Trust me, where color goes, flavor follows.

I'll provide you with my recipe pairing suggestions, as well as many ideas for impressive presentations. Start out by using my recommendations, then experiment on your own. Pay attention to how your plate is composed when dining out. Try different techniques, and don't be afraid when some fall flat. The most wonderful way to learn what works and what fails in terms of presentation and flavor is by cooking and eating! Now, dinner is served.

Hunka Hunka Monkfish

Serves 4

This dish stands out for its gourmet taste and restaurant-quality presentation. Serve it to guests when you want to impress.

3 tablespoons Champagne vinegar

3 tablespoons extra virgin olive oil

1 inch fresh ginger, peeled and sliced

2 garlic cloves, sliced

1 teaspoon red pepper flakes

½ tablespoon chopped flat leaf parsley

½ tablespoon chopped fresh tarragon

4 8-ounce portions monkfish fillets, boneless and skinless

Sea salt, to taste

Black pepper, to taste

2 tablespoons unsalted butter

1 In a small bowl, whisk the Champagne vinegar while slowly drizzling in olive oil. Add the sliced ginger, sliced garlic, red pepper flakes, and fresh herbs.

2 Place the monkfish into a gallon-size storage bag, and completely cover the fish with the marinade. Refrigerate to marinate for

Did You Know This Crap?

Always use fresh, never frozen fish. Fish is especially damaged by freezing because of its high water content. When frozen, that water inside the fish obviously freezes—expanding and tearing the delicate flesh of the fish. When the fish is defrosted, the water just runs out of those tears along with much of the flavor. The texture will now be inferior along with the taste, and whatever cooking process you use will definitely dry out your dinner.

15 minutes, massaging the fish once during those 15 minutes, making sure it is coated evenly. Don't leave it marinating longer that 25 minutes or the vinegar will begin to cook the outside of your fish.

3 Put your 12-inch sauté pan over medium-high heat. Take the monkfish from the marinade and remove the chunks of garlic and ginger. They will not only burn in the hot pan but neither you nor your guests want to bite into a big slice of ginger or garlic. Season each fillet lightly with salt and pepper. While the pan is warming up, add the butter and swirl it around as it melts to coat the pan completely.

4 Once hot, carefully add your fish to the pan making sure the fillets don't touch each other and that the most attractive (the smoothest side) goes down first. Sear the fish on this side for 5 minutes, turn the fillets over, and reduce the heat to medium. Spoon the pan juices over the fish several times while it cooks on this side for 5 minutes without moving it. Since monkfish is thick, you should sear all four sides. Carefully balance the fish on one side and, cook it for 2 minutes and then cook the other

Chefology

MONKFISH

A sneaky little devil, the monkfish lies partially buried on the sea floor twitching to resemble a worm to attract smaller fish into its large, hideous mouth. Also known as angler-fish, frogfish, sea devil, and goosefish, it is low in fat, firm-textured, and has a mild, sweet flavor that has led to the term "poor man's lobster." Once a fish thrown back for his hideous appearance, the monk fish is not only affordable but it comes skinned and ready to go! Super CLK friendly.

side, completely searing the fish, and basting often with the pan juices.

5 Using your chef's knife, cut each portion into ¼-inch slices at an angle. The outside will be crisp and brown, while the inside is soft and sweet. Fan out the slices over the side dishes you have chosen for the plate, perhaps bright steamed vegetables (p. 168) and Sweet Potato Gnocchi (p. 182). Serve immediately. This moist and delicious fish requires no sauce.

Barbequeless Barbequed Salmon

If you have a patio and grill—even a small hibachi grill works great—use it. If not, don't despair. I simply use my large sauté pan on the stove. No need for those special grill pans, all they do is add fake grill marks.

¼ cup rice wine vinegar

¼ cup soy sauce

¼ cup sake

1 tablespoon minced garlic

2 teaspoons peeled and minced fresh ginger

1 tablespoon honey

¼ cup sesame oil

1 cup plus 2 tablespoons olive oil

¼ cup hoisin sauce

3 tablespoons Sambal chili paste

Sea salt, to taste

Black pepper, to taste

4 8-ounce portions salmon fillets, boneless and skinless

1 In a large bowl, whisk together the rice wine vinegar, soy sauce, sake, garlic, ginger, and honey. Slowly drizzle in the sesame oil and then 1 cup of olive oil. Whisk in the hoisin sauce and chili paste. Season to taste with salt and pepper.

2 Place the salmon into a gallon-size disposable bag and coat the fish with just enough sauce to cover. Reserve the rest of the sauce. Refrigerate the salmon to marinate 15 minutes.

3 Put your 12-inch sauté pan over medium-high heat. When the pan is hot, add 2 teaspoons of olive oil and swirl it to coat the pan.

4 Season each fillet lightly with salt and pepper. Carefully add the fish to the pan, making sure the pieces don't touch each other and that the most attractive side (the smoothest-looking side with no gray or fat showing) goes down first. Sear the fish on this side for 7 minutes, turn the fillets over, reduce heat to medium, and cook this side for 7 minutes for medium-rare salmon.

5 Serve immediately sitting atop a tight, round pile of Sautéed Vegetables (p. 170) with extra barbeque sauce drizzled over the fish.

Ya Mon Jerk Chicken

Serves 12

Invite a hungry crew because this recipe makes a lot and is a real crowd-pleaser.

2 tablespoons minced fresh thyme

1 tablespoon ground allspice

1 tablespoon black pepper

2 teaspoons sea salt

1 teaspoon ground cinnamon

a pinch ground nutmeg

1 teaspoon ground ginger

1 teaspoon dry mustard

2 tablespoons orange zest

2 tablespoons lime zest

1 scotch bonnet chili, seeded and minced

2 tablespoons dark brown sugar

3 tablespoons minced garlic

2 cups minced scallions

¼ cup beer (can substitute chicken stock)

¼ cup apple cider vinegar

½ cup extra virgin olive oil

3 pounds chicken thighs, bone in and skin on

3 pounds chicken breasts, bone in and skin on

White Rice (p. 176)

1 In a large bowl, combine all of the dry spices with the zests, chili, sugar, minced garlic, green onion, beer, and vinegar. While whisking the mixture, slowly drizzle in the olive oil to complete the marinade.

2 Place the chicken in the marinade. Thoroughly wash your hands, and massage the marinade into the chicken. Cover the bowl tightly and refrigerate it overnight.

3 The next day, preheat the oven to 350°. Remove the chicken pieces from the marinade, and layer them in your roasting pan. Reserve the marinade. Cover the pan with a lid or foil and place it in the oven to roast 30 minutes. Then remove the cover and allow it to brown for another 30 minutes.

4 While the chicken is in the oven, reduce the marinade by half in a 1-quart saucepot over medium-high heat. Spread What's Right White Rice (p. 176) over a serving tray. Top with chicken. Drizzle the reduced sauce over the jerked chicken.

I Got Sole Meuniere

A very traditional French dish, you should pair sole meuniere (muh-n-YAIR) with very delicate sides such as steamed spinach or a light salad such as This Salad Bites (p. 80), and arrange everything in elegant little separate piles on the plate. Every item on a gourmet French-style plate should coordinate, yet deserves its own gourmet spotlight.

6 tablespoons unsalted butter

6 6- to 8-ounce Dover sole or flounder fillets

Sea salt, to taste

Black pepper, to taste

1 cup all-purpose flour

2 tablespoons olive oil

12 lemon slices, cut extremely thin

4 garlic cloves, smashed

3 tablespoons drained capers

¼ cup freshly squeezed lemon juice

¼ cup dry white wine

½ cup vegetable stock

3 tablespoons chopped flat leaf parsley

1 Place your 12-inch sauté pan over medium-high heat and add 4 tablespoons butter. Season the fillets lightly with salt and pepper, and dredge them in the flour. Once the butter is melted and foaming, dust any excess flour off each fillet as you lay them in the pan, being careful not to let them touch.

Did You Know This Crap?

Real Dover sole has a firm texture and mild, almost sweet, flavor. Imported from Europe, it is rather expensive. Fish bearing its name, such as gray sole or lemon sole, are actually flounder and look and taste similar to Dover sole without the high price tag. Feel free to substitute flounder for any sole recipe.

2 Allow this side to brown for about 4 minutes, and then turn them to cook for another 2 minutes. Move the crispy fillets to a sheet tray, set a piece of foil loosely over them, which will keep them warm without trapping in any steam, and repeat the cooking process with any sole that wouldn't fit in the first batch.

3 When all the fish are crispy, add the 2 remaining tablespoons of butter and 2 tablespoons of olive oil to the sauté pan. Once the butter has melted, add the lemon slices and garlic, allowing the lemon to lightly brown. Place 2 lemon slices over each fillet, and add the capers, lemon juice, and white wine into the sauté pan. Bring this to a boil and reduce by half. Now add the vegetable stock and allow it to thicken for about 2 minutes.

4 Stir in the chopped parsley and taste the sauce to see if it needs salt or pepper. Plate the sole with a tall, thin hill of steamed spinach or even a mound of salad. Spoon the sauce evenly around each fillet and serve immediately.

I'm a Softy
for Soft-Shell Crab

Serves
8

Eat your soft-shell crab from stem to stern with some salad and Chipotle Aioli (p. 198). No chance of crappy little leftovers here!

1½ cups vegetable oil

8 soft-shell crabs, blue crab variety, preferably live and never frozen

Sea salt, to taste

Black pepper, to taste

1 cup all-purpose flour

1 teaspoon Old Bay seasoning

½ teaspoon smoked paprika

1 cup Bock beer (for its caramel flavor to compliment the sweet crab)

3 eggs

2 cups cornmeal

1 recipe Chipotle Aioli (p. 198)

1   You can ask your seafood purveyor to clean your crabs for you, or, if you're feeling assiduous, you can clean them yourself. Put them in the freezer for 10 minutes and they'll go right to sleep. Preheat your oven to the lowest setting possible. Place your 12-inch sauté pan over medium-high heat, and add 1 cup of oil. Take a crab and a pair of kitchen shears and cut off the head, just behind its eyes. On the right and left you will see a pointed flap. Lift

Did You Know This Crap?

Only about 15 percent of a hard-shell blue crab is edible meat. It takes a lot of work to get to those succulent morsels. Thankfully, around the month of May, an astonishing thing happens. The crabs cast off their hard shells to grow larger ones, and while they wait for their new shells, their entire body is soft and *edible!*

that up and scrape away the gills that are inside using the outside of the kitchen shears. Twist the tail until it breaks off and slowly pull it away from the crab to remove the vein. It should slide right out.

2 Season each crab evenly with the sea salt and black pepper. In a medium bowl, combine the flour with the Old Bay seasoning and smoked paprika. In another medium bowl, whisk together the beer and eggs, making an "egg wash." Put the cornmeal in another bowl. Now your "breading station" consists of the seasoned flour, the egg wash, and the cornmeal.

3 Lightly dredge four crabs in the flour, and shake off any excess, then dip them in the egg wash, and then the cornmeal. Use your tongs to carefully place each one top-side down in the hot oil and allow the crabs to gently fry for a full 2 minutes before turning them over. Cook another minute and place the golden brown crabs into your warm oven. Add the rest of the vegetable oil to the pan and repeat this step with the final four crabs. Serve immediately with the crabs sitting high on top of a fresh salad like a Caesar (p. 78) or the Poblano Slaw (p. 84) and dolloped with Chipotle Aioli (p. 198).

Sweet Merciful Scampi

Serves
6

Perfect for summer entertaining, toss this with some Sautéed Vegetables (p. 170) and fresh pasta (p. 172), and serve it with a dry white wine. Buying your shrimp already peeled and deveined not only saves precious time but precious space, dishes, and frustration—making this dish a breeze to prepare.

2 tablespoons extra virgin olive oil

3 garlic cloves, minced

2 tablespoons minced shallots

Sea salt, to taste

Black pepper, to taste

½ cup dry white wine

2 tablespoons fresh lemon juice

8 tablespoons unsalted butter at room temperature

2 pounds jumbo shrimp, peeled and deveined

2 teaspoons chopped flat leaf parsley

2 teaspoons chopped fresh tarragon

1 teaspoon chopped fresh thyme

1 Place your 8-inch nonstick sauté pan over medium heat, and add the olive oil. When it heats up, add the garlic and shallots, season them lightly with salt and pepper, and allow them to soften for about 2 minutes. Add ¼ cup of the white wine, raise the heat to medium-high, and allow it to reduce by half. Stir in 1 tablespoon of the lemon juice and continue boiling until almost all of the liquid is gone. Transfer to a medium bowl and allow it to cool 10 minutes.

Did You Know This Crap?

True scampi are actually a small species of lobster that are a delicacy in the Mediterranean. In the United States, scampi usually refers to a shrimp recipe that includes a sauce made from garlic butter and white wine.

Crappy Little Kitchens

2 Place your 12-inch sauté pan over medium heat and add the butter and half of the seasoned mixture that you made. When the butter has completely melted, toss in the shrimp. Arrange them evenly in the pan and cook on one side for 2 minutes. Turn them over and add the rest of the white wine and lemon juice. Bring this up to a simmer and add the fresh herbs to steep for 1 minute.

3 Use your spider or slotted spoon to remove the shrimp scampi and place them piled high in the center of a serving platter. Then add the remaining seasoned mixture to the pan. Whisk the butter and the mixture together, and taste it to see if it needs more salt or pepper. Pour it over your shrimp and serve immediately.

Make-You-Want-to-Marry-Me Mussels Marinara

Serves 6

With the high quality of canned plum tomatoes, you can whip up a spectacular marinara sauce in almost the amount of time it takes to open a jar of inferior prepared sauce. Not to mention the mussels steam open inside the sauce, making it a one-pot wonder!

5 pounds Prince Edward Sound mussels

3 tablespoons extra virgin olive oil

6 garlic cloves, thinly sliced

35-ounce can crushed plum tomatoes

1 teaspoon red pepper flakes

3 tablespoons chopped fresh basil

Sea salt, to taste

Black pepper, to taste

2 tablespoons chopped flat leaf parsley

1 Discard any mussels that remain open when you lightly tap them against the counter or sink.

2 Put your 12-inch sauté pan over medium-high heat, and add the olive oil. Allow it to heat for a few seconds and add the garlic. Brown it for less than 10 seconds (if it gets too crispy, garlic will have a bitter taste) and add the tomatoes and red pepper.

3 Add all of the mussels to the pan. When the sauce begins to bubble, reduce the heat to medium and cover to cook for 10 minutes.

4 Then remove the lid, and allow the tomatoes to cook down for 5 to 10 minutes while you inspect the mussels. Using your tongs, remove and discard any unopened mussels.

5 Add the basil, season to taste with salt and pepper, and then toss the mussels through the sauce. Pour the entire dish into a serving bowl, garnish with the chopped parsley, and serve immediately.

How to Clean Mussels

Purchase mussels with unchipped shells that are tightly closed. Unwrap and store them in a bowl in the refrigerator so they can breathe until you are ready to prepare them. Before cooking, soak the mussels in fresh water for about 20 minutes. As the mussels breathe, they filter water and expel sand stored inside of their shells. Use your hands to lift the mussels out of the dirty water.

Remove the beard by grasping it with a dry towel and yanking it out toward the hinge end of the mussel, which will prevent the mussel from dying. Scrub the mussels to remove any additional sand or barnacles, then rinse them under cool tap water, and set aside. Dry with a towel before cooking.

Pad Thai Perfection

Quite foolproof and bursting with flavor, make this recipe a regular part of your gourmet cooking rotation.

8 ounces dried wide rice noodles

¼ cup fish sauce

3 tablespoons rice vinegar

2 tablespoons cane sugar (may substitute light brown sugar)

3 tablespoons vegetable oil

2 tablespoons peeled and minced ginger

1 tablespoon minced red Thai chili pepper

2 garlic cloves, minced

1 pound chicken thighs, boneless and skinless, diced

6 cups thinly sliced Napa cabbage

1 bunch fresh cilantro

½ cup toasted and chopped unsalted peanuts

1 lime, cut into wedges

1 Put the rice noodles in a large bowl, and pour over enough boiling water to cover them and soften for about 20 minutes. Put the noodles into your steamer basket and allow them to drain. In a small bowl, whisk the fish sauce, vinegar, and cane sugar until the sugar dissolves, and set it aside.

2 Place your 12-inch sauté pan over medium-high heat and add the vegetable oil. Add the ginger, chili, and garlic, sautéing for 1 minute. Add the diced chicken and sauté until completely cooked, about 2 minutes. Add the cabbage, half of the cilantro, half of the peanuts, and the fish sauce mixture. Sauté for 2 minutes or until the cabbage begins to wilt.

3 Add the noodles, and toss together until they are warm and coated with sauce. Serve immediately. For individual plates, use tongs to twist high piles of the noodles in the center of soup bowls and garnish by pushing a small "bush" of cilantro into the side of each pile of noodles, a lime wedge to the side of that, and an even sprinkling of peanuts over the entire top. The exact same presentation will work for a large platter.

Superlative
Stuffed Chicken Breast

This recipe is quick and easy to prepare with a small list of ingredients that takes you to gourmet heaven even if you think you're living in CLK hell!

3 tablespoons olive oil

4 ounces French goat cheese

4 airline chicken breasts

4 slices Prosciutto, paper thin

8 sage leaves, large

Sea salt, to taste

Black pepper, to taste

1 Preheat oven to 350°. Place your 12-inch sauté pan over medium-high heat and add the olive oil. Cut the goat cheese into fourths. Carefully lift the skin on each breast (just be careful not to remove the skin entirely. You want one side to remain attached) and insert a piece of goat cheese. Top the goat cheese with a slice of Prosciutto and 2 sage leaves, and press the skin back down.

2 Season the top and bottom of each breast with salt and pepper. Carefully lay the chicken pieces skin side down in the sauté pan. Allow the skin to brown for 3 minutes, then turn each breast.

3 Place the entire sauté pan into the oven and cook the chicken for about 15 minutes or until the internal temperature is 165°. Check its temperature by inserting the thermometer into the thickest part of the breast, which should be near the bone that attaches to the breast. Serve immediately alongside just about anything, with no disappointment, but I would recommend a tall, soft pile of the Mashed Magnificence (p. 174) for the breast to lean up against with the wing high in the air, and some braised purple kale tucked into the side.

Chefology

AIRLINE CHICKEN BREAST

This chicken is a fabulous restaurant secret that looks beautiful on the table. It's a large breast with the bone, wing, and skin attached, which add flavor and moisture.

Herb-Crusted Pork Tenderloin

Serves 4

Cutting through the savory outside crust reveals a moist apricot filling making this a feast for the eyes as well as the taste buds. Serve it with Roasted Vegetables (p. 171) and Espagnole Sauce (p. 204) for a standing ovation from even a crappy audience.

¼ cup minced fresh thyme

¼ cup minced fresh rosemary

2 tablespoons minced fresh sage

1 whole pork tenderloin, about a pound

Sea salt, to taste

Black pepper, to taste

1 pound dried apricots, quartered

1 tablespoon finely minced garlic

2 tablespoons finely chopped flat leaf parsley

2 tablespoons olive oil

1 Preheat oven to 350°. Toss the thyme, rosemary, and sage together in a small bowl, set aside. Season the pork with salt and pepper. In another bowl, combine the apricots with the minced garlic and parsley. Place the pork on the cutting board. Insert your bread knife into the short end of the tenderloin. Hold the pork steady with one hand lying flat on top of it, and carefully slice through the center of the pork lengthwise, creating a tunnel of sorts.

2 Stuff the garlicky apricot pieces into one end of the tenderloin tunnel until they start coming out the other side. Store any leftover stuffing in an airtight container in the fridge, and it will stay good for a week. Completely cover the outside of the pork with the herb mixture.

3 Place your 12-inch sauté pan over medium heat (any higher and you will burn your herbs) and add the olive oil. Once the oil begins to shimmer, carefully place the tenderloin in the pan. Allow it to brown for 1 minute, and then turn it slightly. Repeat this until the tenderloin is brown all the way around, and then place it in the oven to finish cooking for 15 minutes, or until it reaches an internal temperature of 165°.

Carefully remove the tenderloin from the pan and place it on a cutting board to rest for 5 minutes. Then cut the tenderloin into ¼-inch disks. Pile the Roasted Vegetables (p. 171) high in the center of four dinner plates. Lean and fan out five disks of pork against the veggies. Drizzle the Espagnole Sauce (p. 204) over the pork, and serve immediately.

Did You Know This Crap?

It's best to let meat "rest" after cooking. Don't worry, the meat isn't tired, it just needs a chance for its juices to redistribute, which will help the meat retain its moisture and flavor when sliced.

Rum-Infused, Carmelized Pork Chops

Serves 4

I like to use a thick cut, bone-in, French-trimmed pork chop. French trimmed means the butcher has already scraped the bone ends clean for you, making an attractive gourmet display. Now you don't have to French the pork chop yourself.

½ cup sugar

1 teaspoon water

¼ cup rum

2 teaspoons olive oil

4 bone-in French-trimmed pork chops, 10 ounces each

Sea salt, to taste

Black pepper, to taste

2 tablespoons butter

1 banana, cut into ¼-inch slices

2 tablespoons heavy cream

1 Preheat oven to 350°. In your 1-quart saucepot, whisk the sugar into the water until it is moist. Place this over medium heat and allow it to simmer. Once the bubbles have begun to get very large and the sugar turns a golden brown color, pull the pot away from the heat and pour in the rum. Reduce the heat to the lowest setting, and return the pot to cook down for about 10 minutes. Give it a good stir to make sure the caramel has come together (it should be thick and uniform at this point), and again remove it from the heat.

2 Place your 12-inch sauté pan over medium-high heat and add the olive oil. Season each side of all four pork chops with salt and pepper. Once the pan has begun to smoke, carefully lay each pork chop into the pan to brown for 5 minutes on this side. Then turn them over, and place the entire pan into the oven to cook for 12 minutes.

3 Take the pan out of the oven and place the chops onto a serving platter. Return the pan to a burner set to medium-high heat and add the butter. Once the butter is melted and foamy, add the slices of banana. Cook them for 2 minutes and then turn them over. Add the

caramel sauce and heavy cream and again bring the sauce to a simmer. Keep the bananas intact by stirring gently around them.

4 Pour the sauce evenly over the pork chops, placing one banana slice on top of each chop, and serve immediately! Family style presentation is easy to plate and works well with a dramatic meal like this. With the pork chops plattered and ready to go, have another platter of roasted brussel sprouts and baby red potatoes (Roasted Vegetables p. 171) that you've sprinkled with red pepper flake to add a spicy contrast to the chop.

Daylight Come and Me Want Pork Stew

Serves 10 to 12

Everything in this dish requires only a rough chop as opposed to a dice, making the preparation a snap, and if you utilize the leftover rice from the night before, it becomes a one-pot wonder.

2 tablespoons olive oil

1½ pounds boneless pork loin, cubed

Sea salt, to taste

Black pepper, to taste

30 ounces black beans, canned and rinsed

2 cups chopped Roma tomatoes (about 3 to 4)

1 cup chopped cherry or red peppers

1 green bell pepper, chopped

1 cup chopped red onion

2 tablespoons minced fresh ginger

3 garlic cloves, minced

1 tablespoon ground cumin

1 plantain, sliced (don't substitute bananas, they won't hold up in this dish)

16 cups chicken stock, or vegetable stock

6 cups cooked jasmine rice (p. 176)

Red pepper flakes, as needed

1 Place your 12-quart stockpot on medium-high heat and add the olive oil. When it begins to smoke, add the pork to brown for 2 minutes while seasoning lightly with salt and pepper. Then turn each piece to brown all over. Add the beans, vegetables, and spices to the pork and sauté for 5 minutes.

2 Toss the plantain slices into the pork mixture and then add the stock. Raise the temperature to high, bring to a boil, and then lower the heat to medium. Simmer for 10 minutes, or until the plantains are soft. Season to taste with salt and pepper.

3 For individual servings, place 1 cup of cooked rice into the center of each bowl and then ladle the stew over the top. Garnish with a pinch of red pepper flakes.

Cherry Cassis Lamb Skewers

Serves 10

This recipe employs prepared veal demi-glace, which you can find in the freezer section of your gourmet market. By dressing up the demi-glace with shallots, garlic, dried cherries, and crème de cassis, no one will ever guess the base of the sauce is store-bought.

1 tablespoon unsalted butter

2 shallots, thinly sliced

2 garlic cloves, minced

1 cup crème de cassis (black currant liquor)

½ cup dried cherries

1 cup prepared veal demi-glace

2 pounds lamb top round

Sea salt, to taste

Black pepper, to taste

36 wooden skewers, 6 inches long

1 Preheat the oven to 400°. Place your 1-quart saucepot over medium-heat and add the butter. Once it is melted, add the shallots and garlic, and sauté until the garlic is soft and the shallots are translucent. Pour in the crème de cassis, raise the temperature to high, and allow it to reduce by half. Then stir in the dried cherries and the demi-glace and reduce to a simmer. Allow this to thicken while you make the skewers.

2 Using a very sharp chef's knife, slice your lamb into ¼-inch thick strips that are about 4-inches long by 1-inch wide. Season the lamb lightly with sea salt and black pepper. Tightly lay the seasoned strips in a single layer on a sheet tray. Place the sheet of lamb into the oven for 6 minutes or until golden brown, and remove them to cool slightly.

3 When cool enough to handle, weave each piece of lamb onto its own skewer. Taste your cassis sauce, and season to taste with salt and pepper. Then use a pastry brush to paint each skewer heavily with sauce. Serve immediately. These tasty morsels also make a great party appetizer.

Swap It

Make this exact recipe using duck breast instead of lamb for an equally impressive result.

Braised Short Ribs Long on Taste

Serves 4

Hope your guests are ready to get their hands dirty! This finger-licking, one-pot wonder is the perfect gourmet dish for hungry company.

¼ cup olive oil

6 pounds English-style beef short ribs

Sea salt, as needed

Black pepper, as needed

2 cups all-purpose flour

2 cups large dice yellow onion

1 cup large dice carrot

1 cup large dice celery

¼ cup minced garlic

½ cup fresh brewed coffee

1 cup red wine

3 cups beef stock

8 ounces canned, crushed tomatoes

¼ cup chopped flat leaf parsley

1 Preheat oven to 400°. Put a Dutch oven or braising pan on the stovetop, heat to medium-high heat, and add the olive oil.

2 Season the short ribs heavily with salt and pepper, then dredge each piece lightly in flour.

3 When the pan begins to smoke, lay one rib on its side into the oil. Let it brown for about 5 minutes, and then turn it slightly to begin browning the other side. Once it is dark on all sides, remove from the pan and begin again. Repeat this for all the ribs, and feel free to brown more than one at a time.

Swap It

IF YOU PREFER more of a barbeque flavor to the traditional braise, substitute a tablespoon of chipotle and ¼ cup of honey for the coffee.

4 Reduce the heat to medium, and add the onion, carrot, and celery. Move the vegetables around in the pan using your heat resistant spatula to make them cook more evenly. When they have begun to soften and caramelize slightly, add the garlic and coffee.

5 Allow this to cook together for 1 minute, then add the wine and bring it up to a simmer. Once it has reduced by half, add the beef stock and crushed tomatoes. Turn off the burner, and bury the ribs in the sauce. Cover the pan and put it in the oven for about 2 hours, or until the meat is peeling away from the bone.

6 Place the ribs on a serving platter, and season the sauce to your taste with salt and pepper. Pour just enough finished sauce over the ribs to cover, and serve immediately. Garnish with lots of freshly chopped parsley. The ultimate one-pot wonder, this dish is perfect served with Mashed Magnificence (p. 174) or Call the Po-Po on This Polenta (p. 177).

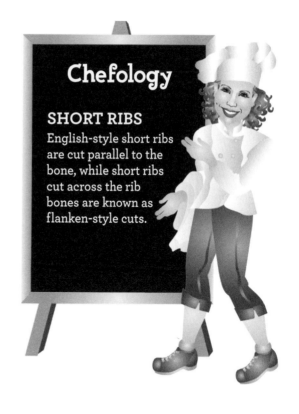

Chefology

SHORT RIBS
English-style short ribs are cut parallel to the bone, while short ribs cut across the rib bones are known as flanken-style cuts.

My Personal Wellington

In a traditional beef Wellington the entire beef tenderloin is wrapped in puff pastry, but I like making beautiful packages that are individual servings. I use phyllo pastry instead of puff, because it's much more CLK friendly since it requires no rolling.

4 beef tenderloin steaks, 8 ounces each

3 tablespoons olive oil, plus more for pan

Sea salt, as needed

Black pepper, as needed

2 ounces foie gras, small cubes

3 tablespoons chopped fresh thyme, plus more for garnish

1 pound cremini mushrooms, finely chopped

8 ounces unsalted butter

1 shallot, sliced

1 box phyllo dough

1 cup Charred Tomato Red Wine Demi Sauce (p. 205)

1 Preheat oven to 350°. Place your 12-inch sauté pan over medium-high heat. Rub some olive oil over the steaks and season them heavily with salt and pepper. When the pan begins to smoke, carefully place each steak into the pan to brown for 2 minutes on one side, and then turn them to brown another 2 minutes on the other side. Repeat this until the tenderloins have become completely seared and crispy on all sides. Move them to a clean plate and refrigerate them.

2 Place your 12-inch sauté pan back over the heat (don't wash it out, those bits have a lot of flavor), and throw in the cubes of foie gras. They will immediately start rendering fat. Add the fresh thyme and mushrooms. Toss this all together and reduce the heat to medium while the mushrooms sweat. Place your 1-quart saucepot over low heat and add the butter and shallot to melt slowly together.

3 Place a small strainer over the saucepot of butter, and once the mushrooms are completely soft, pour them into the strainer to drain. Top your chilling steaks with the strained mushroom mixture and return them to the fridge. Remove the butter from the heat.

4 Open the phyllo dough and unroll it onto a cutting board, and cut it directly down the middle, making two even rectangles. Stack them together, and pull one sheet off the top. Cover the stack with a piece of plastic wrap to keep its moisture in and prevent it from drying out. Using a pastry brush, very lightly paint the piece of phyllo with melted butter. Take another piece of phyllo and place it directly on top of the buttered piece. Butter this layer and continue until you have six layers.

5 Place one-fourth of the mushrooms in a tight circle in the center of the pastry. Set a steak on top of that. Bring up all the sides of the pastry to completely enclose the steak into the pastry like a present, turn it over, and set it on a plate. Repeat steps 4 and 5 with the other three steaks and put the plate in the freezer for 10 minutes to set the phyllo dough and make sure it stays shut when baking.

6 Lightly grease a baking pan with olive oil, place each steak folded side down onto the pan, and place it in the oven for 12 minutes (once rested this should be a good medium rare/medium). Allow them to rest for 10 minutes before cutting a small wedge (or triangle) out of each Wellington. Place the large portions in the center of each dinner plate. Spoon a circle of the Charred Tomato Red Wine Demi off to one side and place the small wedge of Wellington in the center of that circle. Lightly sprinkle the plate with chopped thyme and serve immediately.

The Perfect Pot Roast

Serves
10

A Sunday favorite, this complete meal requires only one pot. Buying a roast with no bone means less cooking time and easy slicing.

3 tablespoons olive oil

Sea salt, as needed

Black pepper, as needed

3- to 4-pound boneless
    rump roast

¾ cup dry sherry

¼ cup Dijon mustard

2 tablespoons minced
    fresh rosemary

2 tablespoons minced
    fresh thyme

2 cups beef stock

2 tablespoons
    Worcestershire sauce

3 tablespoons
    cornstarch

¼ cup water

2 celery stalks, leaves
    attached

2 carrots, large

5 garlic cloves, smashed

1 pound new potatoes

12 ounces baby carrots

1 cup fresh pearl onions

1 Preheat oven to 350°. Place a Dutch oven over medium-high heat and add the olive oil. Heavily salt and pepper the roast on all sides. Once the pan has begun to smoke, carefully place the roast into the pan to brown for 5 minutes on one side. Then, turn it onto the next side for another 5 minutes. Repeat this for every side of the roast until it is completely browned, and then remove it from the pan. If your pan is too small to conveniently sear on all sides, use your torch to brown the sides with wonderful results. The idea is to brown the entire roast to seal in the juices.

2 Deglaze the pan by adding the dry sherry to the hot pan and stirring to loosen the tasty brown bits, and allow it to reduce. Use a pastry brush to lightly coat the roast with Dijon mustard, and then season it with the fresh herbs.

3 When the sherry has reduced by half, add the beef stock and Worcestershire, allowing it to come to a simmer. In a very small bowl, whisk the cornstarch and water together to make, what we call in chef circles, a slurry. Pour this into the stock and again allow it to all come to a simmer. Remove the pan from the heat.

4 Place the celery stalks and large carrots in the slurry and crisscross them to make a platform for the roast. Add the smashed garlic, and lay the roast on top of the vegetables.

5 Arrange the potatoes, baby carrots, and onions around the roast, cover the pan, and put the entire thing in the oven for 1½ to 2 hours or until it reaches an internal temperature of 150°. Season the sauce to taste with salt and pepper. Serve the roast in the center of a large platter with the small vegetables surrounding it. Pour some of the sauce over the entire dish, and serve the rest on the side.

Snake-Charmin' Moroccan Lamb Chops

Serves 8

By marinating the chops overnight, this dish requires only 2 minutes of total cooking time. Serve with sautéed diced eggplant and tomato (Sautéed Vegetables p. 170) tossed with the Saffron Couscous (p. 186), and you'll have an authentic gourmet Moroccan meal.

2 tablespoons olive oil

4 lamb racks, 5 to 6 bones each

Sea salt, as needed

Black pepper, as needed

3 tablespoons fresh lemon juice

¼ cup extra virgin olive oil

2 teaspoons ground coriander

1 teaspoon ground allspice

1 teaspoon ground cumin

1 cup chopped fresh mint

2 tablespoons minced fresh ginger

2 tablespoons minced garlic cloves

1 Place your 12-inch sauté pan over medium-high heat and add the olive oil. Season each whole rack heavily with salt and pepper. Once the pan has begun to smoke, carefully place one rack, fat side down, into the pan and allow it to brown on this side for 5 minutes or until extremely crispy. Then rotate it to the other side to brown. Remove it from the pan to cool and repeat this with the other 3 racks. Once they cool, cut down each bone making individual "chops." Hold the rack by one of the bones allowing the bottom to rest on the cutting board. In short sawing motions, run your chef's knife along each bone while trying to cut each as evenly in size as you can. Place the lamb chops in plastic storage bags.

2 In a medium bowl, add the lemon juice and slowly whisk in the extra virgin olive oil. Whisk in the coriander, allspice, cumin, mint, ginger, and garlic. Pour this marinade all over the lamb chops, and place them in the refrigerator for a minimum of 4 hours.

3 Preheat the oven to its lowest setting, set an oven-safe dish or sheet tray inside, and place your 12-inch sauté over medium-high heat. Shake off excess marinade from each chop,

but allow most to remain. Once the pan is hot, carefully sear each lamb chop for 1 minute on each side, and then place them in the oven to stay warm while you repeat with remaining chops. When every lamb chop is crispy, they are ready to serve. For family-style presentation put a bowl of the Saffron Couscous (p. 186) topped with Sautéed Vegetables (p. 170) in a bowl and set it on the end of a platter. Cascade the lamb chops, slightly over lapping them as they build up toward the bowl of couscous and vegetables. Serve immediately.

Feta and Fennel Stuffed Leg of Lamb

Ask your butcher for a shortened leg of lamb (known as the shank half), with the shank end of the bone left in, and the hip end of the bone removed. The meat will come wrapped around the bone. With the hard work completed by the butcher, preparing the recipe is a snap. This meal comes out so juicy and colorful, your guests will be rendered speechless until the end of the meal. Make sure you only use this on big occasions, not crappy little ones, because it's tough to ever top the experience.

¼ cup olive oil

1 fennel bulb, thinly sliced, reserve green tops

1 red onion, thinly sliced

4 garlic cloves, thinly sliced

2 cups chopped Swiss chard, tender greens

Sea salt, to taste

Black pepper, to taste

3½ to 4 pound shank half of a leg of lamb, bone left in

½ cup crumbled feta cheese

½ cup chopped kalamata olives

¼ cup finely chopped fresh mint

¼ cup finely chopped fresh oregano

½ cup red wine

1 Place your 12-inch sauté pan over medium-high heat and add half of the olive oil. When it begins to smoke add the fennel and red onion, sautéing until they become translucent. Toss the garlic through the mixture and then add the Swiss chard. Turn the heat down to medium while the Swiss chard wilts into the onions and fennel. Season the mixture to taste with salt and pepper. Remove from the heat to cool.

2 Unroll the leg of lamb and evenly sprinkle the inside of the meat with the crumbled feta and olives. Spread a thick layer of the sautéed fennel and greens over the feta and olives. Roll the lamb closed, making sure all the stuffing stays in, and secure it with toothpicks. Season the outside of the lamb with salt, pepper, chopped mint, and oregano, wrap the whole thing with plastic wrap, and place it in the fridge overnight.

3 One hour or so before you want to serve, preheat the oven to 375°, place your roasting pan over medium-high heat, and add the second half of the olive oil. When it begins to smoke, carefully place the leg of lamb into the pan to brown on one side for 3 minutes. Once it is crispy, roll it over to brown on the next section for 3 minutes. Continue this way until you finally roll it onto that last side, pour in the red wine, and place the pan into the oven immediately. Roast the leg for 30 minutes or until the internal temperature is 135°.

4 Set the lamb aside to rest for 15 minutes, and place the pan of wine back on medium heat to reduce it into a thick sauce. This won't take very long, so watch it closely, and give it a stir occasionally to keep it from burning to the bottom. On your serving platter, make a bed of the reserved fennel greens, place the leg of lamb in the center, and pour the red wine sauce over the top. Serve immediately with Roasted Vegetables (p. 171). For presentation purposes, it's quite exciting to carve the meat at the table. Place the leg of lamb on its side on a cutting board. Starting on the outside, cut thin slices parallel to the bone until you reach the bone. Transfer the slices to a platter and start again on the opposite side, continuing until the bone is naked!

Chefology

TRUSS
To truss involves using string, skewers, or toothpicks to hold food together so it maintains its shape (and its stuffing) while cooking.

Chiles Rellenos

The chile relleno, literally means "stuffed chile," and is a dish of Mexican cuisine that originated in the city of Puebla. It consists of a roasted fresh poblano pepper (the poblano pepper is named after the city of Puebla) that is stuffed with cheese, rice, or meat. This recipe utilizes my special gourmet method for creating perfectly cooked rice every time.

¼ cup plus 3 table-spoons olive oil

6 poblano peppers

1 yellow onion, small dice

1 tablespoon smoked Spanish paprika

1 cup long grain rice

½ cup golden raisins

¼ cup chopped pecans

1⅓ cup vegetable stock

Sea salt, to taste

Black pepper, to taste

¾ cup Queso fresco, white cheese

2 cups self-rising cake flour with a pinch of salt

4 cups corn oil

8 egg whites

½ teaspoon cream of tartar

1 Preheat oven to 400°. Place the poblanos on a sheet tray and drizzle ¼ cup of olive oil over them. Roast them for 15 to 20 minutes or until they have begun to blacken and blister. Remove them with your tongs, place them in a mixing bowl, and cover with plastic wrap to steam.

2 Place your Dutch oven over medium-high heat and add 3 tablespoons of olive oil. Once it begins to smoke, quickly sauté your onions until they begin to soften, and add the smoked paprika. Carefully add the rice, toss it all together, and allow the rice to brown for 5 minutes, stirring occasionally. Add the raisins and pecans, and then pour in the stock, and season to taste with salt and pepper. Allow this to boil, remove from the heat, cover and stick in the oven for 45 minutes exactly.

3 Once the peppers are cool, carefully peel off their skins. Make a 2-inch slit in the side and carefully remove as many seeds as you can, trying not to tear the pepper. Stir ½ cup of cheese into the rice mixture. Cup the pepper in one hand with the slit side up and open. Use your other hand to gently stuff ¼ to ⅓ cup of

rice filling into each pepper. Close the slit in each pepper with two or three toothpicks. Save any leftover rice filling for adding to the Tomato and Avocado Fritatta (p. 144) for breakfast in the morning. Wash and dry the Dutch oven for the next step.

4 Dredge each stuffed pepper in the flour. Place the Dutch oven over medium-high heat, and add the corn oil. In a large bowl, whisk the egg whites and cream of tartar until the whites form soft peaks. Roll a pepper in the egg whites, and carefully drop it into the oil. Repeat with two other peppers. You should be able to fry three at a time. Turn them often, and fry them for about 5 minutes or until golden brown. Gently remove them and place them on paper towels to drain. Repeat with the rest of the peppers, and carefully remove the toothpicks when the peppers are cool enough to handle.

5 Serve warm, drizzled with Mexican Mole Sauce (p. 212) and garnished with the Queso fresco crumbled over the top. If you like, top it with some Latin Salsa Verde (p. 218) or Pico de Gallo Salsa (p. 215).

Did You Know This Crap?

Never try to simulate the flavor or texture of meat in a vegetarian dish, because if you do you will fail.

Leaning Tower of Tofu Lasagna Stacks

Serves 4

I've received rave reviews for this vegetarian entrée in my restaurants. The tofu doesn't replace the meat in this recipe. It is a high-protein, low-fat substitute for the noodles!

½ cup olive oil

16 ounces extra firm tofu

Sea salt, to taste

Black pepper, to taste

2 eggs

¼ cup milk

1 cup all-purpose flour

1 cup plain bread crumbs

2 tablespoons unsalted butter

2 cups (about 8 ounces) sliced cremini mushrooms

1 zucchini, halved lengthwise and sliced

1 recipe Mighty Marinara Sauce (p. 210)

6 ounces provolone cheese, thinly sliced

¼ cup thinly sliced fresh basil leaves

1 Preheat the oven to its lowest setting. Place your 12-inch sauté pan over medium-high heat, and add the olive oil. Make ¼-inch slices down the length of the tofu and lay the slices on paper towels to absorb any moisture. Gently salt and pepper each tofu "noodle" and cover with more paper towels.

2 Whisk together the eggs and milk in a medium bowl to make an egg wash. Line up a medium bowl of flour, the egg wash in the middle, and a medium bowl of bread crumbs on the end. Lightly dredge the tofu in the flour, dip it in the egg wash, and then coat it in the bread crumbs. Drop a pinch of bread crumbs into the hot oil. If it fries rapidly then the oil is ready. Carefully place four pieces of tofu in the olive oil and fry until golden brown (about 2 minutes), turning once to brown the other side. Place each finished noodle on a baking sheet lined with paper towels in the oven to stay warm and drain.

3 Rinse your 12-inch sauté pan, dry it off, return it to medium-high heat, and add the butter. When it has melted, toss in the mushrooms to coat them with butter, lightly season with salt and pepper, and turn down the heat to medium to allow the mushrooms to sweat.

After about 10 minutes, when the mushrooms have released their liquid, add the zucchini and sauté until it also becomes soft. Season the mixture to taste with salt and pepper and turn out onto clean paper towels to get rid of the liquid we sweated out. Again wash this pan for the next step.

4 Turn the oven up to 350°. Lay four tofu slices in the sauté pan. Top each tofu slice with some mushroom and zucchini mixture, marinara sauce, and a slice of provolone. Then place another tofu "noodle" on each stack and layer with the other ingredients.

5 Place the pan in the oven until the cheese has melted and the marinara is hot, about 10 minutes. Use your spatula to center each stack on a dinner plate and garnish with a sprinkling of fresh basil.

BYOM (Bring-Your-Own-Margarita) Mushroom Tamales

Serves 10

My mushroom tamales receive rave reviews in my restaurants as well as my home. This gourmet meal can become the reason you have the gathering. Throw a tamale-making party, and don't forget the margaritas!

36 large dried cornhusks

½ ounce dried porcini mushrooms

8 ounces cremini mushrooms caps, sliced

1 cup unsalted butter, softened

¼ cup finely chopped yellow onion

1 garlic clove, minced

8 ounces shitake mushrooms, sliced

1 teaspoon crumbled dried epazote

Sea salt, to taste

Black pepper, to taste

2 cups finely ground dry corn masa harina (Mexican flour)

½ teaspoon baking powder

1 teaspoon sugar

2 cups mole sauce (p. 212)

1 Cover the cornhusks with hot water to soften for 30 minutes. Drain and cover the husks with a damp towel. Soak the dried porcinis in 1 cup of hot water for 30 minutes. Reserve the soaking liquid, but squeeze as much water as possible from the porcinis, slice them, and place them in a bowl with the sliced cremini mushrooms. Place a paper towel, like a filter, into the top of a measuring cup. Slowly pour the mushroom liquid through the paper towel to filter out any grit, and reserve the strained liquid.

2 Add 2 quarts of water to your 12-quart stockpot and put it over medium-high heat.

Swap It

If you can't find epazote at your local market, substitute dried cilantro.

3 Place your 12-inch sauté pan over medium heat and add ¼ cup of the butter. Once melted and foamy, add the onion and garlic. Sauté until the onions have become translucent. Add the mushrooms and epazote and toss the entire mixture together, sautéing for 5 minutes. Season the mixture to taste with salt and pepper. Pour in the porcini water, bring it to a simmer, and drop the heat to low so it can reduce slowly.

4 Combine the masa, baking powder, sugar, and ½ tablespoon of salt into a large bowl. Stir in 1½ cups of hot water and then ¾ cup of softened butter. Fold the dough over and over in the bowl until it becomes smooth.

5 Flatten 3 tablespoons of corn dough into the center of a cornhusk (½-inch thick). Cover it with 1 tablespoon of mushrooms and then 1 tablespoon of Mole sauce. Fold the top and the bottom of the husk closed, then fold closed the right side to completely cover the filling. Roll the whole tamale over onto the left flap encasing the tamale like a package. Repeat until you run out of mushrooms.

6 Raise the temperature under the stockpot to high. Fill the

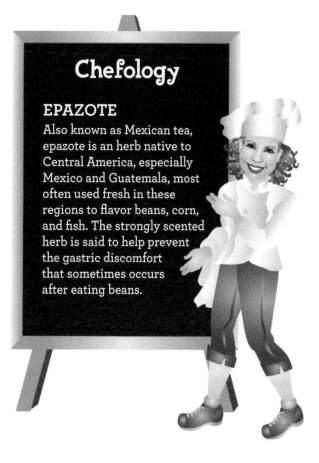

Chefology

EPAZOTE
Also known as Mexican tea, epazote is an herb native to Central America, especially Mexico and Guatemala, most often used fresh in these regions to flavor beans, corn, and fish. The strongly scented herb is said to help prevent the gastric discomfort that sometimes occurs after eating beans.

steamer basket with tamales by standing them up on end. Cover and steam the tamales for 40 minutes. Remove them from the basket with tongs, stack them high on a platter, and serve immediately with extra Mole sauce and the Spanish rice (minus the pecans and raisins) from the Chili Relleno (p. 134) in bowls nearby. You can individually wrap the leftovers tightly in foil and freeze them, but they never last that long in my Crappy Little Kitchen.

Barbequeless Barbequed Salmon, p. 106

My Personal Wellington, p. 126

Make-You-Want-to-Marry-Me Mussels Marinara, p. 114

Snake Charmin' Moroccan
Lamb Chops, p. 130

I Got Sole Meuniere, p. 10

Superlative Stuffed
Chicken Breast, p. 117

I'm a Softy for Soft Shell Crab, p. 110

Mushroom Tamales, p. 138

Oh Lamby Boy! p. 152

Assorted Frittatas, p. 144–146, 148

Eat Your Vegetables Risotto, p. 162

Dignified One-Pot Creations

The most CLK friendly dishes are those that can fit all that crap into one pot! To be a true one-pot wonder, everything should be tossed, cooked, and even served in one single pot. This method of cooking cuts down on dishes (obviously), as well as prep time, and requires little space and only one burner for gourmet cooking results. This chapter explores some of my favorite only-one-pot-needed dishes that guarantee a spectacular gourmet finish.

Classic one-pot wonders span the globe—the French have cassoulet (a rich, slow-cooked bean stew or casserole originating from France's Languedoc region in the south), the Spanish have paella (a rice dish that originated in its most recognized form near the eastern coast of Spain's Valencian region), and the Indians have kema (a hearty casserole of lentils, potatoes, tomatoes, and curry served all over India), to name a few. One-pot wonders run the gourmet gamut of flavors, textures, and even shapes and sizes.

You'll love the ease of preparation and gastronomic genius you'll achieve with the use of only one pot!

Tomato and Avocado Frittata with Cracklin' Corn Bread

Serves 4

You can find the ingredients for this recipe precut at your local market to save time on dicing. Or, make this dish when you have leftover salsa or Pico de Gallo Salsa (p. 215). Just add the sliced avocado.

2 tablespoons extra virgin olive oil

½ cup diced yellow onion

1 clove garlic, minced

½ cup diced Roma tomatoes

Sea salt, to taste

Black pepper, to taste

6 eggs, beaten

1 avocado, sliced

Corn bread (see recipe that follows)

1 Preheat oven to 300°, and place your 8-inch nonstick sauté pan over medium heat. Add the olive oil to the pan and allow it to heat up. Put the onion in the pan and lightly sauté until it starts to soften and change color. Then add the garlic and tomato and continue to sauté another 2 minutes. If the elements start to caramelize or turn brown, turn down the heat a bit. Add a pinch of salt and pepper to season.

Did You Know This Crap?

A frittata is an open-faced Italian omelet traditionally filled with leftover meats, vegetables, and cheeses. You can use any variety of ingredients that inspire you, making a frittata the perfect dish for your CLK.

2 Pour in the eggs, and move the onion, garlic, and tomatoes around to disperse them evenly in the pan. While the eggs begin to cook, arrange your avocado slices on the top of the frittata fanning them around into a complete circle. Allow it to cook this way for 1 minute.

3 Sprinkle another pinch of salt and pepper evenly over the eggs and avocado. Put the entire pan in the center of the oven for 10 minutes.

4 Using a potholder or dry towel, remove the pan from the oven and run a heat-resistant spatula around the outside of the frittata to make sure it will release. Slide it out onto your cutting board and, using your chef knife, cut it like a pizza.

5 Serve warm, with 2 wedges of frittata fanned over a slice of warm, buttered corn bread.

To make the Cracklin' Corn Bread:

2 cups flour

1 teaspoon baking soda

1 tablespoon baking powder

2 tablespoons sugar

1 tablespoon salt

1½ cups cornmeal

3 cups buttermilk

4 eggs

½ cup melted butter

1 Preheat oven to 350°. In a large bowl, add all of the dry ingredients and whisk to sift them together. Make a well in the center and pour in the buttermilk, eggs, and melted butter. Whisk to make a smooth batter.

2 Spray a 9 x 13-inch cake pan (disposable is fine) with cooking spray and fill with the corn batter. Bake until golden brown on top and a butter knife inserted into the center comes out clean, about 15 minutes.

3 Cut into whatever shapes you fancy.

The-Morning-After Pasta Frittata

Serves 4

This recipe calls for angel hair pasta, but please use whatever pasta you have available. Always toss your leftover pasta with a touch of olive oil before you store it in the refrigerator or you'll wake up to a brick of pasta. This recipe is so good, you may want to make pasta just to serve this recipe.

2 tablespoons extra virgin olive oil

1 cup cooked pasta

1 clove garlic, minced

¼ cup freshly grated parmesan

Sea salt, to taste

Black pepper, to taste

6 eggs, beaten

¼ cup Boomin' Basil Pesto (p. 220), as garnish

1 Preheat oven to 300°, and place your 8-inch nonstick sauté pan over medium heat. Add the olive oil to the pan and allow it to heat up. Toss the pasta with the garlic and half of the parmesan cheese; add it to your pan and season with a pinch of salt and pepper. Use your tongs to move the pasta around in the pan to cook it evenly.

2 When the pasta is golden brown, pour the eggs in and around the pasta. Allow it to cook for 1 minute.

3 Sprinkle another pinch of salt and pepper evenly over the eggs. Put the entire pan in the center of the oven for 10 minutes.

4 Using a potholder or dry towel, remove the pan from the oven and run a heat-resistant spatula around the outside of the frittata to make sure it will release. Slide it out onto a cutting board, and, using your chef's knife, cut it like a pizza.

5 Serve warm, fanned over a serving platter, and drizzled evenly with pesto.

Uncle Chris's Squash

Serves 8

This recipe was inspired by Uncle Chris and serves as a staple at all my family's Thanksgiving feasts. Some may think using garlic powder is less than gourmet, however, it provides a more consistent flavor in this dish than bits of fresh garlic.

1 pound green zucchini, ½-inch thick pieces, cut into quarters

1 pound yellow squash, ½-inch thick pieces, cut into quarters

4 Roma tomatoes, medium dice

2 teaspoons garlic powder

2 teaspoons sea salt

1 teaspoon black pepper

2 eggs

2 cups shredded sharp Cheddar

⅓ cup bread crumbs

2 tablespoons butter

1 Preheat oven to 350°. Toss the zucchini, yellow squash, tomatoes, garlic, salt, pepper, eggs, cheese, and ¼ cup of the bread crumbs all together in your greased 9 x 13-inch baking dish (a disposable baking dish will work beautifully if you'd rather toss the dish than wash it).

2 Sprinkle the rest of the bread crumbs on top and drop tiny pieces of butter over the bread crumbs.

3 Bake the casserole for about 30 minutes or until the top is golden brown. Allow it to rest about 20 minutes before serving warm directly out of the dish.

Gourmet Casseroles

It is important to have a few quality casserole recipes up your sleeves for pot lucks and the holidays. Thus far, I haven't held a single Thanksgiving in my home (thank you Crappy Little Kitchen!), but I always show up somewhere else with lots of food. Besides, it's mighty convenient to bring a casserole. Serve your creation directly out of its baking dish. What could be more CLK friendly?

The Mean Green Frittata

Serves
4

Brussels sprouts are a fantastic seasonable vegetable, best when purchased from late August through March when they are small and lime green. Don't miss out on this delectable dish. Fresh Brussels sprouts are nothing like the stinky mush you were forced to eat as a kid.

2 tablespoons extra virgin olive oil

1 cup cleaned and quartered fresh Brussels sprouts (small)

2 cloves garlic, minced

½ teaspoon red pepper flakes

Sea salt, to taste

Black pepper, to taste

6 eggs, beaten

2 slices whole wheat toast, buttered

1 Preheat oven to 300°, and place your 8-inch nonstick sauté pan over medium heat. Add the olive oil to the pan and allow it to heat up. Sauté the Brussels sprouts with the garlic and red pepper flakes, and season them with a pinch of salt and pepper.

2 When the Brussels sprouts are bright green and begin to soften, pour in the eggs. Disperse the Brussels sprouts evenly in the pan. Allow the eggs to cook for 1 minute.

3 Sprinkle another pinch of salt and pepper evenly over the eggs. Put the entire pan

Swap It

Use fresh broccoli or cauliflower instead of the Brussels sprouts, following this recipe exactly.

in the center of the oven for
10 minutes.

4 Using a pot holder or dry towel, remove the pan from the oven and run a heat-resistant spatula around the outside of the frittata to make sure it will release. Slide it out onto a cutting board and, using your chef knife, cut it like a pizza.

5 Serve warm, with 2 pieces of frittata fanned over a half-piece of toast (cut on a diagonal).

Did You Know This Crap?

Brussels sprouts are part of the cruciferous or mustard family, which includes broccoli, cabbage, and cauliflower. They taste a lot like cabbage but have a slightly milder flavor. Look for bright green Brussels sprouts without black spots, holes, or yellow leaves. The stem ends should be clean and white. They should not have a strong smell, so avoid sprouts with a pronounced cabbage odor. To wash properly, drop the sprouts into a bowl of lukewarm water and leave them there for ten minutes. Rinse in fresh water, trim the stem ends, but don't trim them flush with the bottom of the sprouts, because you don't want the outer leaves to fall off during cooking. If you cook Brussels sprouts whole, cut an X about one-sixteenth of an inch into the stem end to ensure faster and more even cooking. Insert a knife tip into the stem end to determine if done; the stem end will be barely tender.

Let's Get Hoppin' Braised Rabbit

Serves 6

Don't shy away from rabbit just because you like the Easter bunny. Ask your butcher to order it for you. Expand your culinary tastes; you won't be sorry! Cut the celery, carrots, and onions thick so they don't cook too quickly.

¼ cup olive oil

6 rabbit hind quarters (legs plus thighs)

Sea salt, to taste

Black pepper, to taste

2 cups large dice yellow onion

1 cup large dice carrot

1 cup large dice celery

¼ cup chopped garlic

Chipotle, minced (depending on the heat you want, use 1 tablespoon for mild, 2 tablespoons for medium, and ¼ cup for hot)

2 tablespoons ground cumin

3 cups vegetable stock

15 ounces canned, crushed tomato

¼ cup chopped fresh cilantro

1 Preheat oven to 400°. Put your Dutch oven on the stove, turn to medium-high heat, and add the olive oil.

2 Season the rabbit evenly with salt and pepper.

3 When the olive oil has begun to smoke slightly, use your tongs to lay one leg, skin side down into the oil. Let it brown for about 1 minute, and then turn it slightly to begin browning the other side. Once it is golden on both sides, remove from the pan and put on a clean plate, and begin again. Repeat the process for all the legs and thighs, and feel free to brown more than one at a time.

Swap It

If you can't bring yourself to buy rabbit, you can substitute chicken legs and thighs in this recipe.

Three should fit comfortably in a Dutch oven without overcrowding.

4 Reduce the heat in your pan to medium, and add the onion, carrot, and celery. Move them around in the pan using a heat-resistant spatula so they cook evenly. When they have begun to soften and caramelize slightly, add the garlic, chipotle, and cumin. Allow this to cook together for 1 minute, seasoning lightly with salt and pepper.

5 Add the stock and tomato, and bring it up to a simmer. Turn off the heat, and bury the rabbit beneath the sauce in the pan. Sprinkle with a pinch more of salt and pepper. Cover the pan, and put it in the oven for about 1 to 1½ hours. When the meat is peeling away from the bone, the dish is ready.

6 You can serve the quarters as entrée portions with Mashed Magnificence (p. 174) smothered in the vegetable-rich braising liquid. Or you can let the rabbit cool slightly, and shred the meat off the bone. Toss it with sauce and pasta, or serve it wrapped in corn tortillas with sauce on the side. Garnish with lots of chopped cilantro.

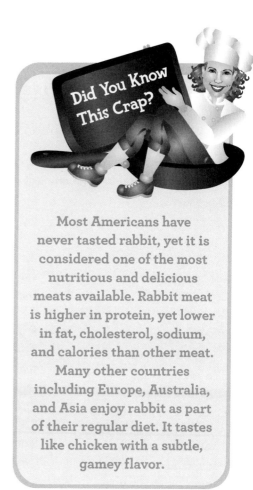

Did You Know This Crap?

Most Americans have never tasted rabbit, yet it is considered one of the most nutritious and delicious meats available. Rabbit meat is higher in protein, yet lower in fat, cholesterol, sodium, and calories than other meat. Many other countries including Europe, Australia, and Asia enjoy rabbit as part of their regular diet. It tastes like chicken with a subtle, gamey flavor.

Oh Lamby Boy!

This shepherd's pie recipe is high on the wow factor. The presentation is outstanding, and no one will know how easy this one-pot wonder is to prepare!

¼ cup olive oil

4 lamb shanks, ½ pound each

Sea salt, to taste

Black pepper, to taste

¼ cup all-purpose flour

2 cups large dice yellow onion

1 cup, peeled and cut in one-inch lengths on the bias, carrots

1 cup, cut in one inch lengths on the bias, celery

4 tablespoons unsalted butter

¼ cup chopped garlic

2 tablespoons chopped fresh thyme

2 tablespoons chopped fresh rosemary

2 bay leaves (preferably fresh, but can substitute dried in equal portion)

4 cups vegetable stock

3 pounds small Yukon gold potatoes, halved

¼ cup chopped fresh Italian parsley

1   Preheat oven to 400°. Put your Dutch oven on the burner, heat to medium-high heat, and add the olive oil.

2   Season the lamb shanks heavily with salt and pepper; don't worry about over-seasoning. Dust them lightly with flour.

3   When the olive oil begins to smoke slightly, use your tongs to lay the lamb shanks on their sides into the oil without overcrowding them. Let them brown for about a minute, and then turn them slightly to begin browning the next section. Once they are brown on all sides, remove them from the pan. Repeat this for all the shanks.

4   Reduce the heat in the pan to medium, and add the onion, carrot, and celery. Move them around in the pan using a heat-resistant spatula to help cook them evenly. When they have begun to soften and caramelize slightly, after about 10 minutes, add the butter and allow it to melt. Add the garlic, thyme, rosemary, and bay leaves and allow this to cook together for 1 minute.

5   Add the stock and bring it to a boil. Turn off the burner, arrange the 4 shanks in the middle of the pan and surround with the

How to Cut on the Bias

"On the bias" means cutting on a slight angle. Lay the vegetable horizontally on the cutting board and, with your non-knife-wielding hand, hold it down close to the end where you'll begin cutting. Curl your fingers so that the tips are tucked under and the knuckles point outward—in the chef world, this is called the "claw grip." Hold the blade of your chef's knife against the vegetable at a 45-degree angle. Begin slicing slowly toward your holding hand, making sure to keep your fingers tucked in. Reposition your "claw grip" to make sure it doesn't wind up a few fingers too short!

fingerling potatoes. Sprinkle a pinch more salt and black pepper over the potatoes. Cover the pan and put it in the oven for about 3½ hours. When the meat peels away from the bone, the lamb is ready!

6 Present this right in the roasting pan. Garnish with lots of chopped parsley, and place it in the center of the table.

Chefology

LAMB SHANK

Cut from the arm of shoulder, lamb shank contains the leg bone and part of the round shoulder bone and is covered by a thin layer of fat and fell (a paperlike covering). Lamb shank is usually prepared by braising or by cooking in liquid.

When the Saints Come Marchin' In Gumbo

Serves 8

All good Cajun cooking begins with its very own holy trinity: onion, celery, and bell pepper. You can buy the vegetables pre-diced and use peeled and de-veined shrimp to save on preparation and clean up time. Everything gets thrown into the same pot, so there's no mess in your Crappy Little Kitchen.

½ cup butter or bacon fat

½ cup all-purpose flour

5 garlic cloves, chopped

1 medium yellow onion, large dice

2 stalks celery, large dice

1 medium green bell pepper, large dice

Sea salt, to taste

Black pepper, to taste

12 cups chicken stock or vegetable stock

1 bay leaf (preferably fresh, but can substitute dried in equal portion)

15 ounces diced tomato, canned

2 tablespoons Worcestershire sauce

2 tablespoons Tabasco

½ teaspoon cayenne pepper

1 tablespoon chopped fresh thyme

8 ounces fresh okra, sliced thin

1 pound select crabmeat

1 pound raw, peeled, and de-veined shrimp (medium size, about 30–35 shrimp)

1½ teaspoons gumbo filé

¼ cup chopped fresh Italian parsley, plus more for garnish

1 recipe steamed white rice (p. 176)

1 Warm the butter or fat over low heat in your 12-quart stockpot. Lightly sprinkle in the flour while whisking it all together. Allow the flour to brown over a low heat, stirring often, until it is the shade of peanut butter. This may take about

Did You Know This Crap?

Okra comes from a plant by the same name that produces an edible pod. It originated in Africa and was brought to America by slaves. Buy brightly colored pods less than four inches long that are not bruised or soft. Okra with a very sticky texture means it is too ripe.

45 minutes but is very important to the flavor of your roux or base.

2 Add the garlic, onion, celery, and bell pepper, allowing them to cook and soften for 10 minutes, releasing flavor into your roux. Season lightly with salt and pepper to help sweat the vegetables.

3 While whisking, slowly add the chicken stock. Keep whisking to incorporate all of the roux and liquid together so you won't have lumps.

4 Now add the bay leaf, tomato, Worcestershire, Tabasco, and cayenne pepper, and bring to a simmer. Simmer slowly uncovered for about an hour, stirring often.

5 At this point, season to taste with the salt and pepper. Then add the thyme, okra, crab, and shrimp. Continue to simmer for about 20 minutes or until the shrimp is cooked.

6 Add the gumbo filé and parsley, and remove the pot from the heat. Taste the gumbo, if you want it kicked up a notch, add a little more cayenne pepper. Put a tall pile of rice in the center of your serving bowls and ladle the warm gumbo around

Chefology

GUMBO FILÉ
Gumbo filé is the powdered dried leaves of the sassafras tree. It tastes similar to root beer. An essential flavoring and thickening ingredient of gumbo and other Créole dishes, it becomes stringy with cooking. That's why we add it when the cooking process is complete.

the outside, creating a bright white island. Garnish each island with a pinch of chopped parsley.

Swap It

If you have guests who are allergic to shellfish or would simply prefer chicken, substitute two pounds of diced, boneless chicken thighs for the crab and shrimp.

The Best Paella You'll Ever Eat

Paella is named after the large flat pan that it is traditionally cooked in, but don't buy a special pan that you'll have to store in your Crappy Little Kitchen! I find my 12-inch sauté pan works perfectly, but mine has very deep sides. If yours doesn't, you can use your Dutch oven.

¼ cup extra virgin olive oil

8 ounces chicken thighs, boneless and skinless

8 ounces shrimp, raw, peeled, and deveined (21 to 25 per pound)

Sea salt, to taste

Black pepper, to taste

2 cups small dice yellow onion

2 tablespoons minced garlic

1 cup small dice poblano pepper

2 red chili peppers, thinly sliced

¼ teaspoon saffron threads

2 cups medium-grain rice

½ cup dry white wine

4 cups chicken stock

8 ounces diced tomatoes, canned

4 sprigs fresh thyme

1 pound littleneck clams, cleaned (see How to Clean Mussels p. 115, skipping the step to remove the mussel beard since clams are beardless)

1 pound mussels, cleaned (see p. 115)

¼ cup chopped fresh Italian parsley

Lemon wedges for garnish

1 In your 12-inch sauté pan, heat the olive oil over medium-high heat. Dice the chicken into 1-inch cubes. Season the chicken and shrimp with salt and pepper. Using your tongs, brown the chicken on all sides. After the chicken is golden brown, add the shrimp and sauté until they just begin to curl and change color. Remove them both, and put them on a clean plate.

2 Turn the heat down to medium and add the onion, garlic, poblano, red chili, and half the saffron. Cover the pan and allow the vegetables to sweat for 5 minutes. Add the rice and sauté it all together for 10 minutes. Season it lightly with salt and pepper.

3 Sprinkle the rest of the saffron threads into the white wine while you sauté the rice. Then pour the wine and saffron into the sauté pan. Allow the wine to cook and reduce until it is almost gone.

4 Add the chicken stock, tomato, and thyme. Stir gently and bring to a simmer, then carefully season to taste with salt and pepper. Place the clams and mussels on top of the simmering liquid and cover tightly. Keep covered until the shell-fish open completely and the rice is tender and forming a crispy crust on the bottom, about 15 minutes. Remove from heat, and discard any clams or mussels that didn't open.

5 Generously sprinkle the dish with parsley, and decorate with the lemon. Serve directly out of the pan.

Swap It

I recommend Spanish Bomba or American CalRiso rice for paella, but you will also have good results with Italian Carnaroli and Japanese sushi rice. Do not use long-grain or parboiled varieties, which do not absorb as much liquid as short- or medium-grain rice.

Wreck-Proof Spinach Risotto

Serves 6

There is just no way to rush risotto without negatively affecting your final product. The constant stirring of the cooking rice is what develops the starches to create that deliciously creamy consistency. This glowing example of a one-pot wonder was probably invented in a Crappy Little Kitchen.

2 tablespoons extra virgin olive oil

4 tablespoons unsalted butter

¾ cup minced yellow onion

2 tablespoons minced garlic

Sea salt, to taste

Black pepper, to taste

2 cups Arborio rice

⅓ cup dry white wine

6 cups vegetable stock

½ cup heavy cream

1 pound baby spinach

2 teaspoons lemon zest

⅓ cup freshly grated pecorino Toscano cheese

1 In your 12-quart stockpot, heat the olive oil and 2 tablespoons of butter over medium heat. Add the onion and garlic. Stir, season lightly with salt and pepper, and allow them to soften but not brown. This should take about 6 minutes.

2 Stir in the rice and continue stirring until the edges of the rice become translucent; this will take 1 to 2 minutes. Pour in the wine and continue stirring until it evaporates.

Did You Know This Crap?

Arborio rice is a high-starch, short-grained type of rice that is the traditional choice for making classic Italian risotto.

3 Season lightly at this point with salt and pepper, and add just enough stock to cover the rice. Bring the temperature up to a high simmer, and stir constantly until all the liquid has been absorbed. Continue cooking, adding just enough stock each time to cover the rice and never stop stirring, or your starch will not develop. This should take about 30 to 45 minutes. When the rice is almost completely cooked or al dente (it will be translucent on the outside with a tiny pearl of white in the middle), stir in the heavy cream, spinach (saving 10 spinach leaves for garnish), and lemon zest, and continue stirring until all of the spinach has softened into the rice.

4 Remove from the heat, stir in the last 2 tablespoons of butter, and ½ of the Pecorino cheese. Taste, and if necessary, add salt and pepper. Stack the 10 spinach leaves and roll them into a thin cigar. Slice it thinly, making long skinny strips, which are called chiffonade in chef-speak. Pile the risotto high in the center of a serving platter, or put oval-shaped scoops in the center of individual plates. Garnish with Pecorino and the chiffonade of spinach and serve immediately.

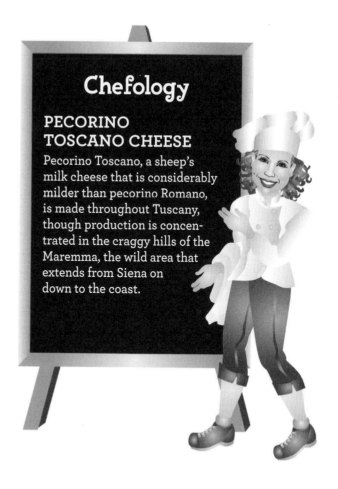

Chefology

PECORINO TOSCANO CHEESE

Pecorino Toscano, a sheep's milk cheese that is considerably milder than pecorino Romano, is made throughout Tuscany, though production is concentrated in the craggy hills of the Maremma, the wild area that extends from Siena on down to the coast.

Island Hopping Seafood Risotto

Serves 6

This is the most memorable meal I had in Italy on the Isle of Capri. Even a Crappy Little Kitchen can transport you to the crystal blue waters of the Italian coast.

¼ cup extra virgin olive oil

1 pound shrimp, raw, peeled, and deveined (21 to 25 per pound)

2 ounces bay scallops

8 ounces calamari, sliced into rings

Sea salt, to taste

Black pepper, to taste

4 tablespoons unsalted butter

1 cup white part only, sliced and cleaned leeks (save ¼ cup of the dark greens for later)

2 tablespoons minced garlic

2 cups Arborio rice

⅓ cup dry white wine

6 cups fish or vegetable stock

⅓ cup freshly grated Parmigiano-Reggiano

1 In your 12-quart stockpot, heat the olive oil over medium heat. Season the shrimp, scallops, and calamari with salt and pepper. Once the pot is very hot, carefully use your tongs to brown the seafood on all sides. Don't let them cook all the way through, just brown, and then remove them from the pot, and place on a clean plate.

2 Add 2 tablespoons of butter to the stockpot and allow it to melt. Toss in the white leeks and garlic. Stir, season lightly with salt and pepper, and allow them to soften but not brown, for about 6 minutes. Stir in the rice and continue stirring until the edges of the rice become translucent; this will take 1 to 2 minutes. Pour in the wine and continue stirring until the wine evaporates.

3 Season lightly at this point with salt and pepper, and add just enough stock to cover the rice. Bring the temperature up to a high simmer, and stir constantly until all the liquid has been absorbed. Continue cooking, adding just enough stock each time to cover the rice and never stop stirring or your starch will not develop. This should take about 25 to 30 minutes. When the rice is almost completely cooked, or al dente (it will be translucent on

the outside with a tiny pearl of white in the middle), add the last bit of stock and remove from the heat.

4 Stir in the cooked seafood, the last 2 tablespoons of butter, and half of the Parmesan cheese. Taste and, if necessary, add salt and pepper. Either pile it high in the center of a serving platter, or put oval shaped scoops in the center of individual plates. Garnish with Parmesan cheese and the thinly shaved leek greens and serve immediately.

Eat Your Vegetables Risotto

Serves 6

This is a truly perfect meal for any vegetarian friends or family coming for dinner. It's flavorful, colorful, and extremely impressive. Baby artichokes don't need to be boiled separately, which is why this dish represents an outstanding one-pot wonder!

6 baby artichokes, small and tender

2 lemons

¼ cup extra virgin olive oil

1 cup white and green parts, sliced and cleaned leeks

1 cup small dice carrots

2 tablespoons minced garlic

Sea salt, to taste

Black pepper, to taste

1½ cups sliced cremini mushrooms

2 cups Arborio rice

⅓ cup dry white wine

6 cups vegetable stock

1 cup frozen peas

2 tablespoons unsalted butter

⅓ cup freshly grated pecorino Toscano cheese

1 Pull your trash can over to your cutting board area, because you're going to have to work fast to prevent the baby artichokes from turning brown. Slice the lemon in half. Go through the entire pile of baby artichokes slicing off the bottom stem (in a large artichoke this is edible, but not so in the baby) and then chopping off the top half-inch of the pointy leaves. Rub the cut ends of the artichokes with the lemon; the juice will keep them from oxidizing and turning brown. Squeeze the rest of the lemon juice into a medium-size bowl.

2 Now stand over the trash can and, just as if you were shucking corn, peel off the dark, coarse outer leaves. When you reach the tender and pale greenish-yellow leaves, move to the next artichoke. If there are any tough, dark green spots on what's left of the stem, trim it off with your knife. Cut each of the artichokes into quarters lengthwise, and put them into the lemon juice. Add enough cool water to the bowl to cover the artichokes and set them aside.

3 In your 8-quart stockpot, heat the olive oil over medium heat, and add the leeks, carrots, and garlic. Stir, season lightly with salt and pepper, and allow them to soften but not

How to Clean Leeks

Because they grow in sandy soil, leeks are difficult to clean. Cut off the very dark green top and the rootlet at the bottom, and the slice the leek in half lengthwise. Thinly slice the leeks and put them directly into a container of water large enough to hold the leeks while covered with water. Stir them around in the water and then allow the leeks to float to the top. The sand will float to the bottom and you can skim your fresh and clean leeks right off the top.

• •

brown. This should take about 6 minutes. Add the mushrooms, season lightly with salt and pepper, and cover for 5 minutes to sweat them.

4 Uncover, stir in the rice, and continue stirring until the edges of the rice become translucent, which will take 1 to 2 minutes. Pour in the wine and continue stirring until it evaporates. Drain the lemon water off your baby artichokes and add them to the rice.

5 Add just enough stock to cover the rice. Bring the temperature up to a high simmer, and stir constantly until all the liquid has been absorbed. Continue cooking, adding just enough stock each time to cover the rice, and never stop stirring or your starch will not develop. This should take about 25 to 30 minutes. When the rice is almost completely cooked or al dente (it will be translucent on the outside with a tiny pearl

of white in the middle), add the peas and the last bit of stock. Remove from the heat when the last of the stock is absorbed.

6 Stir in the butter and half of the pecorino cheese. Taste and, if necessary, add salt and pepper. Either pile the risotto high in the center of a serving platter with the baby artichokes arranged around the outside, or put tall scoops in the center of individual plates with three baby artichokes fanned over the top. Garnish with pecorino and serve immediately.

Lasagna Love Affair to Remember

We are using fresh pasta and vegetables, which have so much natural water, that there's no need to preboil the pasta. That saves us a pot on our Crappy Little stove! If you can't find fresh lasagna noodles, just substitute with dry pasta that you boiled in supersaturated salt water (to prevent sticky noodles), and follow the cooking time on the package.

2 cups Spicy Pomodoro Sauce (p. 211)

2 pounds fresh lasagna noodles

2 pounds fresh whole milk ricotta

2 pounds fresh baby spinach

1 pound zucchini squash, ½-inch quarters (cut ½-inch disks and then cut those into quarters)

1 pound eggplant, cut in ½-inch cubes

Sea salt, to taste

Black pepper, to taste

8 ounces fresh mozzarella, thinly sliced

10 basil leaves

1 Preheat oven to 350°. In a 9 x 13-inch baking dish, (a disposable baking dish is fine) spread a thin layer of Pomodoro, and lay down the first layer of pasta. Cut it to size if it doesn't fit. Spread ¼ cup of the Pomodoro over the layer of pasta. Next, spoon ¼ of the ricotta into dots over the sauce and layer with ¼ of the spinach, zucchini, and eggplant. Lightly season the layer with salt and pepper.

2 Repeat the layers of pasta, sauce, ricotta, and vegetables (with light salt and pepper) 3 more times. End with a fifth layer of pasta and a little more sauce. Arrange your thin slices of mozzarella and basil leaves over the top of the lasagna.

3 Bake the lasagna for 20 minutes until the sauce and cheese are bubbling hot and golden brown, and let it sit to rest 20 minutes before serving warm, directly out of the dish.

Artful Accompaniments

The perfect gourmet meal requires well-prepared accompaniments commonly known as side dishes, so don't neglect this essential element. In this section, I'll share my chef secrets for foolproof side-dish preparations that are ideally suited for your Crappy Little Kitchen. From basic cooking methods for vegetables, pasta, rice, and potatoes to elegant recipes for goat cheese soufflés and seafood timbales, you'll glean a wealth of restaurant-proven knowledge that will compliment your entrées and turn your ordinary meals into extraordinary masterpieces.

Don't make a crappy meal by messing up your side dishes. Follow my advice for perfectly prepared accompaniments to round-out every meal.

Veggies Steamed and Simple

I find that floral vegetables, like broccoli, broccoli rabe, cauliflower, artichoke, and asparagus taste best and achieve the perfect texture when steamed. You only need salt and pepper to season steamed vegetables, but my recipe includes onion, garlic, and thyme, which are added to the water used for steaming. They are called aromatics because they add flavor through the steaming process but are not eaten. This gourmet trick will enhance the flavor of any vegetable you steam. Finish the veggies by tossing with a few tablespoons of butter or olive oil. You only need your stockpot/steamer basket combo to create perfectly steamed veggies making this another CLK-friendly one-pot wonder.

4 cups vegetable stock
or water

1 yellow onion,
chopped

3 garlic cloves,
smashed

10 fresh thyme sprigs

2 pounds vegetables to
be steamed, cut to
be the same size

Sea salt, to taste

Black pepper, to taste

3 tablespoons extra
virgin olive oil

1 Add the stock, onion, garlic, and thyme to your 12-quart stockpot and place it over high heat. You can cover the pot to speed the process.

2 Once it simmers, reduce the heat to medium, place your steamer basket filled with vegetables over the stockpot, and cover with either a lid or aluminum foil. Be careful to lower the temperature again if the stock starts to boil. Anything above a simmer will cause the outside of the vegetables to cook faster than the inside.

Allow the vegetables to steam until just tender. Start checking them for doneness when the vegetables first turn a vibrant color. To test, spear a piece with a fork, if it goes in easily, it's done. Season them lightly with sea salt, freshly cracked black pepper, and a drizzle of extra virgin olive oil or some butter.

Better-Believe-It Braised Vegetables

Serves
4 to 6
Sturdy vegetables like escarole, Swiss chard, kale, and even fennel do very well when braised. Braising vegetables involves cooking them quickly with a little fat and then simmering them with liquid in the same pan, which makes preparation in a CLK a breeze. Simmering southern style greens will take out their natural bitterness, and this cooking method works great for fibrous vegetables like Swiss chard, because the longer cooking time tenderizes them.

3 tablespoons unsalted butter

4 garlic cloves, smashed

2 pounds vegetables to be braised, washed thoroughly, and cut into large chunks (about 1- to 2-inch squares)

Sea salt, to taste

Black pepper, to taste

⅔ cup chicken stock or white wine

1 Place your 12-inch sauté pan over medium heat. Add the butter and garlic and allow the butter to melt slowly and infuse with the garlic flavor.

2 Once the butter has completely melted and the garlic has begun to soften, add as much of your vegetables as will comfortably fit in the sauté pan in a thick single layer. Turn the heat up slightly to medium high. Carefully turn the vegetables over and, as they shrink, add more vegetables if necessary. Season lightly with salt and pepper and continue turning them while they wilt down.

3 Once completely softened, add the chicken stock or wine and reduce the heat to medium. Allow this to simmer for several minutes, until most of the liquid has evaporated out. Taste the vegetables at this point to see if they need more salt or pepper. Remove from heat and serve as a large island in a family style serving dish with braising liquid surrounding it, or as a tiny island in the center of a dinner plate topped with your protein.

Show-Your-Sensitive-Side Sautéed Vegetables

Serves 4 to 6

Delicate vegetables like summer squash, spinach, bell peppers, mushrooms, and eggplant shouldn't be abused by long cooking methods. The trick to perfect texture and flavor is to sauté cook them on high heat for a short period of time. Any way you look at it, sautéed vegetables are CLK friendly for their quick cooking in a single pan.

3 tablespoon olive oil

4 garlic cloves, smashed

2 pounds vegetables to be sautéed, cut to be the same size either on the bias or in cubes

Sea salt, to taste

Black pepper, to taste

1 Place your 12-inch sauté pan over medium-high heat and add the olive oil. Once it begins to smoke, add the garlic cloves, and stir them around in the hot oil while they brown. Remove the garlic and then add the vegetables, using your tongs to arrange them in an even layer.

2 Allow them to brown 1 minute, and then toss them around to finish cooking for one more minute. Season to taste with salt and pepper. When you taste them to check your seasoning, they should be crisp on the outside and tender on the inside. Serve immediately as a high stacked "great wall" of vegetables on a family style platter, or tossed together with some pasta.

Rock-'n'-Roasted Vegetables

Almost any vegetable can be roasted, save for delicate greens. Certainly fingerling potatoes, sweet potatoes, and baby red potatoes are naturals in a roasting oven, but so are rutabaga, Brussels sprouts, and carrots. The trick is usually to blanch them first, which is the first step in this recipe. By blanching them gently, we foolproof the cooking method. All that's left to do is crisp them in the oven!

2 pounds vegetables to be roasted, cut if necessary into large, even pieces like wedges

3 tablespoons kosher salt

3 garlic cloves, smashed

5 fresh rosemary sprigs

¼ cup extra virgin olive oil

Gray sea salt

Black pepper, to taste

1 Preheat the oven to 500°. Fill your 12-quart stockpot one-quarter of the way up with water, and place it over high heat. Add the vegetables to the water, and then 3 tablespoons of kosher salt. If the water doesn't completely cover the vegetables, add more until it does. Bring the water to a boil with the vegetables already in the pot. If you boil the water first and then add the vegetables, the outside will cook too quickly.

2 Once the vegetables are barely tender when stuck with a knife (the knife should go in easily but should not release from the vegetable), drain them using your steamer basket. Pour them out over a sheet tray, add the garlic cloves and rosemary, and drizzle the olive oil evenly over the whole thing. Use your tongs to move the vegetables around, coating everything with oil. Season evenly with gray sea salt and some pepper.

Put the tray of vegetables into the oven and roast until everything is golden brown. This should take about 15 to 20 minutes. Serve them piled high in the center of a family style platter with a bouquet of fresh herbs planted in one corner.

Peter Piper Picked a Pasta

Serves 2 to 4

It is wonderful that you can buy fresh pasta in the refrigerator case at the market, so take advantage of it. Everything from spinach to whole wheat pasta is available fresh, but if you aren't able to find the variety or shape you want in fresh, quality dried pastas are just as good. Simply remember to add a little cooking time to dried pastas, and taste them to make sure they're done. A fabulous side dish, estimate 3 ounces of pasta per person. If pasta is the main dish, plan on 4 to 6 ounces per person. The only chance you have to flavor your pasta is through the salting of your water, so make sure to do this or your pasta will be crappy! You'll find a plethora of recipes in the sauce section that work well on pasta, but fresh pasta is also superb simply tossed with butter and a good Parmesan cheese. Using your stock pot/steamer basket combo turns this into a CLK-friendly one-pot wonder.

¼ cup sea salt

8 ounces pasta

1 Put your 12-quart stockpot over high heat and fill it halfway with water. When bubbles begin to form at the bottom, add a pinch of salt. If it sinks to the bottom, the water isn't hot enough, so wait 5 more minutes and try again. If a cloud forms as the salt is dissolved, the water is ready. Now you may continue adding salt, a little at a time, until the cloud no longer forms and the salt settles at the bottom. This means that your water is "supersaturated" and perfectly salted.

2 When the water is at a full boil, add the pasta. How long it takes to cook the pasta depends on the size and whether it is fresh or not. Fresh pasta will cook very quickly and should only need about 5 minutes, but you should check it after 2 minutes by taking a bite. Dried pasta takes a little less than 10 minutes. Follow the directions on the package for al

dente (firm) pasta. You never want to overcook pasta. After 5 minutes, pull a piece of dried pasta out of the water, and cut it in half or simply take a bite. If it is still white or crunchy in the middle, let it cook and test after one minute. Continue testing in one minute increments.

3 Once the pasta is cooked, drain it in your steamer basket. Add immediately to whatever sauce it is being served with, and toss together. If you allow the pasta to finish inside the sauce, not only will the sauce prevent it from sticking together, but the warm pasta will absorb some of the sauce while coating itself very well.

4 For the butter and parmesan version, melt 4 ounces (1 stick) of butter in a sauté pan. Toss the pasta through the butter, and then sprinkle with ½ cup freshly grated parmesan cheese. You can toss in Sweet Merciful Scampi (p. 112) or Sautéed Vegetables (p. 170).

5 To serve, use your tongs to grab the portion of pasta you want, dangle just over the center of the plate. Set it down while twisting your tongs as if using a screw driver, continuing to twist as you lift the tongs away, and your pasta will be presented in a beautiful coil. If not using a sauce immediately, toss the pasta with a little extra virgin olive oil, and this will help keep the pasta from sticking together.

Mashed Magnificence

Serves
6 to 8

You'll love the extra buttery flavor that shines through in these taters. They mash up in no time, so don't save this recipe for Thanksgiving. Make it anytime!

2 pounds Idaho
potatoes

¼ cup sea salt

8 ounces unsalted
butter

¼ cup heavy whipping
cream

Sea salt, to taste

White pepper, to taste

1 Put your 12-quart stockpot over high heat and fill it halfway with water. Stand over your trash can and peel the potatoes, then immediately place them in the stockpot with the water as soon as they are peeled. This will keep your potatoes from turning brown. Once they are all peeled, take them out one at a time, quarter them, and place them back in the water.

2 When the water comes to a boil, add the salt and turn the heat down to a simmer. After simmering for 20 minutes, test to see if the potatoes are cooked by squeezing one with your tongs. If it crushes easily, you're ready to mash.

3 Once the potatoes are cooked, carefully drain them into your steamer basket. Then return the potatoes to the stockpot, and place the pot in the sink. Cut the butter into cubes, and drop the cubes of butter into the hot potatoes. Using your whisk, mash up the potatoes with the butter. As the butter is incorporated and all the lumps are mashed out, the potatoes are going to become light and fluffy.

4 Whisk in the heavy cream and season to taste with sea salt and white pepper. White pepper is the secret ingredient for most

restaurant mashed potatoes, if you've ever wondered why the ones at the gourmet restaurant taste so much better than the ones you make at home. A little bit goes a very long way, so start small, you can always add more. Serve immediately, or wrap tightly in a bowl and place over a pot of lightly simmering water to hold warm for up to an hour.

When serving, pile the whipped masterpiece high on a serving platter, or fill a large dinner spoon and use another spoon about the same size to scrape it off the spoon onto the center of a dinner plate. It should come off looking like an egg (also called a quenelle shape) to be topped or surrounded by any protein.

Swap It

Starchy potatoes are what you would normally use with mashed potatoes, but it's not a necessity. Red creamer potatoes make excellent mashed potatoes, and so do purple potatoes (or Peruvian blues), Yukon golds, and even sweet potatoes. Put a handful of peeled garlic cloves in enough olive oil to cover them, and simmer until soft. Add this mellow sweet garlicky goodness to any potato about to be mashed for spectacular results.

Try adding finely chopped chives, rosemary, sage, or whatever your favorite herb to what will be your family and friends new favorite side dish.

What's Right White Rice

Serves
6 to 8

Perfectly cooked rice is a wonderful thing to master, and this recipe is truly foolproof. For an added boost of flavor, use chicken or vegetable stock instead of water, add ½ cup finely chopped onion, or simply fold in some unsalted butter when you open the lid.

2⅔ cups water

2 cups jasmine rice

1 tablespoon sea salt

1 Preheat oven to 350°. Add all three ingredients to your 12-quart stockpot, and place it over high heat. When bubbles begin to form at the bottom, cover it with a fitted lid or a tight wrapping of foil.

2 Place the covered stockpot of rice into your oven to bake for 45 minutes exactly. Pull it out when your timer dings, and keep it tightly closed until you're ready to serve.

Swap It

If you'd like to substitute brown rice, simply increase the amount of water to 3 cups.

Call the Po-Po on This Polenta

Serves 10 to 12

Polenta is a popular side dish in many gourmet restaurants. No one would ever expect the simplicity involved in its preparation.

3 cups whole milk

2 cups chicken stock

1 bay leaf, fresh (or substitute 1 dried)

½ yellow onion, peeled and left intact

Sea salt, to taste

Black pepper, to taste

1½ cups polenta, or yellow cornmeal

4 tablespoons unsalted butter

1 cup diced Roma tomatoes (about 2)

½ cup freshly grated Parmesan cheese

¼ cup thinly sliced fresh basil

1 Place your 12-quart stockpot over medium heat, and add the milk, chicken stock, bay leaf, and onion. Allow this to come to a boil. Remove the bay leaf and onion half. Season the liquid to taste with salt and pepper. Begin whisking and drizzle in the polenta slowly, while stirring constantly.

2 Once all of the polenta is added, it should begin to thicken and bubble. When this happens, reduce your heat again to low, and stir continually for at least 5 minutes. Check to see if it needs more salt or pepper.

3 Remove from heat and stir in the butter, tomato, and Parmesan cheese. Serve immediately, poured in the center of a large serving platter and garnish with the fresh basil, or scoop individual portions onto your dinner plates. Pour leftovers into an oiled loaf pan, cover, and refrigerate. The polenta will become solid overnight. Remove it from the loaf pan, and you can slice it into beautiful layers that can be snacked on cold or heated up with a little leftover tomato sauce for a wonderful lunch.

Butternutty Squash Bread Pudding

Serves 8

A big hit when I brought this to Thanksgiving, who could say no to bread pudding or butternut squash? Make it a day ahead, and reheat it in the microwave on Thanksgiving. Saving oven space on Thanksgiving can be a crappy little lifesaver.

1 loaf (about a pound) focaccia bread, cubed

3 tablespoons unsalted butter

2 shallots, sliced

3 tablespoons chopped fresh thyme

3 tablespoons chopped fresh rosemary

2 pounds butternut squash

1⅓ cup heavy cream

4 eggs

½ teaspoon cinnamon

½ teaspoon nutmeg

1 teaspoon sea salt

½ teaspoon black pepper

1 Preheat oven to 350°. Place the cubed bread on a sheet tray and toast until golden brown, about 10 minutes. Place your 12-inch sauté pan over medium-high heat and melt 1 tablespoon of butter. Once it has melted, sauté the shallots until they begin to brown, then remove them from the heat. Add the thyme and rosemary and stir the mixture together.

2 Place the butternut squash on a large cutting board, and use your chef's knife to cut off the stem and the very bottom to create a

Swap It

Focaccia or even brioche work perfectly for this recipe, but definitely choose any soft bread lying around the house. Crusty breads don't absorb the custard as well, and no one wants dry, crappy bread pudding!

flat surface on the top and bottom. Now cut in half, through the waist. Run your knife along the outside, peeling off the skin of the squash. Use a spoon to scoop out the seeds after both halves are peeled. Now cut them into small cubes.

3 Toss the squash together with the shallots and herbs in the sauté pan, and add the bread cubes. Use the remaining 2 tablespoons of butter to lightly coat the inside of a 9 x 13-inch baking dish (disposable is fine). Evenly layer the squash mixture inside the baking dish.

4 Pour the heavy cream into your 1-quart saucepot, and heat it over medium heat. In a medium bowl, whisk together the eggs, cinnamon, nutmeg, salt, and pepper. When the cream comes to a boil, carefully pour it over the egg mixture while whisking to temper or prevent the eggs from curdling. Pour this custard evenly over the squash and bread. Bake for 45 minutes or until it is golden brown and the custard is set. Serve warm cut into fun shapes including triangles or squares to prevent waste, but for an elegant presentation, diamond-shaped servings are the way to go.

Get Your
Goat Cheese Soufflés

Serves
6

Unlike a conventional cheese soufflé, this recipe is not only full of flavor but tangy and incredibly stable (that's chef-speak for its ability to stay nice and puffy). It can be made ahead of time and reheated quite easily, so it is extremely CLK friendly!

6 tablespoons
    unsalted butter

4 eggs

4 tablespoons
    all-purpose flour

1½ cups whole milk

8 ounces soft goat
    cheese

1 tablespoon freshly
    grated Parmesan
    cheese

2 teaspoons Dijon
    mustard

2 tablespoons chopped
    fresh chives

1 tablespoon chopped
    flat leaf parsley

Sea salt, to taste

Black pepper, to taste

½ lemon, juiced

1 Preheat oven to 350°. Use 2 tablespoons of butter to coat the inside of six soufflé cups (You can find disposable aluminum cups in the grocery store. 10-ounce or 5-inch aluminum baking cups are what you're looking for), and put them in the refrigerator. Separate each egg, placing four eggs whites into a medium-size bowl and let them come to room temperature, which will take about 10 minutes. Put three egg yolks in the refrigerator, and discard the fourth yolk.

2 Place your 1-quart saucepot over medium heat and add 4 tablespoons of butter. When the butter has melted, stir in the flour, and cook for 2 to 3 minutes. Stirring constantly, gradually drizzle in the milk, and allow it to come to a boil. Reduce the heat to medium-low, and simmer 5 minutes, stirring regularly.

3 Melt the goat cheese and Parmesan into the milk sauce. Once it becomes smooth again, stir in the mustard, chives, and parsley. The sauce should be thick like glue. Remove from heat and allow the sauce to cool for a few minutes.

How to Separate Eggs

When I separate eggs, I like to crack one in half and hold it over a clean container to catch the white. Slowly separate the halves allowing only the whites to fall into the container. Carefully transfer the yolk to the other half of the shell (without breaking the yoke), and the rest of the white should fall away into the bowl. This method will get easier with practice (that means you have to try it more than once). You can also crack the egg and drop the yoke onto the fingers of one hand that you've positioned over the egg white container. Open your fingers slightly to allow only the white to fall through. The whole, separated yolk should be resting in your fingers.

4 Once cool enough to touch, season it to taste with salt and pepper. Stir in the three egg yolks, and place the bowl in the refrigerator. Now return to your egg whites, which will be easy to beat at room temperature. Add the juice of half a lemon to your egg whites and beat until they reach stiff peaks. You'll know they are ready when you can turn the bowl upside down and the stiff peaks stay in place.

5 Add the cheese mixture into the egg whites and gently put your spatula in the center of the bowl. Pull toward yourself scraping the spatula along the bottom. When the spatula breaks the surface of the batter, turn the bowl about an inch, and start again. Each time you pull up and then drop the spatula back into the center, you will be folding in the egg whites to the batter. Continue around the bowl one time or you will deflate all of your egg whites, and immediately divide the soufflé batter among the buttered dishes. Place the dishes onto a baking pan and place them in the oven. Bake for 20 minutes, or until the soufflés are golden brown and firm to the touch.

6 If serving immediately, leave them in the cups for a soufflé effect, or pop them out and store in an airtight container until ready to reheat. To reheat, place the soufflés in a warm oven for a few minutes. To serve, position a soufflé at 12 o'clock on a dinner plate and your protein such as Sole Meuniere (p. 108) in the bottom left at 8 o'clock with your vegetable (steamed baby carrots p. 168, for example) in the bottom right at 4 o'clock pointing toward the fish. Very French (very gourmet) presentation!

Better-Than-Nookie Sweet Potato Gnocchi

Serves
6 to 8

I use a freezer bag as a pastry bag for this recipe, making it a super example of Crappy Little Kitchen ingenuity. I love this recipe topped with Spicy Pomodoro (p. 211), and then garnished with slivers of basil and good Parmesan cheese.

1 pound sweet potatoes

½ cup extra virgin olive oil

½ cup all-purpose flour

½ cup freshly grated Parmesan cheese (save some for garnish)

Sea salt, to taste

Black pepper, to taste

1 egg yolk

Basil, sliced for garnish

1 Preheat oven to 350°. Rub the sweet potatoes with olive oil, put them on a baking sheet, and place them in the oven. They should roast about 30 minutes. Remove the sweet potatoes from the oven. Hold a hot potato with a dry, clean kitchen towel, and carefully cut a slit running the length of it. Then squeeze the flesh into a medium-size bowl. Repeat with the remaining potatoes.

2 Use your whisk to mash any lumps out of the roasted sweet potatoes. Fold in the flour and Parmesan cheese using the traditional folding technique. Don't overmix the dough once the flour is added or you will make the dough tough. Season to taste with salt and pepper, and then mix in the egg yolk. Refrigerate for an hour to chill and set up to a firmer texture.

3 Place your 12-quart stockpot with built-in strainer over high heat and fill it halfway with water. When the water begins to boil, add 2 tablespoons of sea salt.

4 Place your 12-inch sauté pan on medium-high heat. Then take your gnocchi dough out of the refrigerator and put it into a freezer

bag. Push all of the contents into a bottom corner of the bag and cut a centimeter-size hole into that corner.

5 Standing by the boiling water, squeeze lightly on the freezer bag to force out some dough, about 1 centimeter in length. Use your chef's knife to cut each dumpling, making it fall into the boiling water. Use half of the bag of dough in this fashion.

6 When those dumplings begin to float in the boiling water, add ¼ cup of olive oil to the 12-inch sauté pan. Carefully strain the gnocchi from the stockpot by slowly lifting out the strainer and allowing all of the water to drain out. Carefully pour the dumplings into the sauté pan. Move them around slightly to make sure they brown evenly. When golden brown, transfer them to your serving platter.

7 Repeat steps 5 and 6 with the dough remaining in the freezer bag. Pile the gnocchi high down the center of a large serving platter, top with Spicy Pomodoro (p. 211) and garnish the center of the plate with sliced basil and grated Parmesan cheese

Chefology

GNOCCHI
Gnocchi (pronounced NYOH-kee) is Italian for "dumplings" and can be made from potatoes or flour. Gnocchi are generally shaped into little balls, cooked in boiling water, and served with butter and Parmesan or a savory sauce, but they can also be chilled, sliced, and either baked or fried.

Under-the-Sea Timbales

Anyone will enjoy the beauty of this stunning dish, which is a special treat for seafood lovers. Try topping this with Lemon Tarragon Sauce (p. 192) as a side dish or with Béarnaise Sauce (p. 197), and serve it as an appetizer course. To reheat, simply pop it in the microwave for 1 to 1½ minutes. Super CLK friendly.

4 tablespoons unsalted butter

1 pound small shrimp, peeled and deveined

1 pound bay scallops

2 eggs, 1 whole plus 1 yolk

½ cup whole milk ricotta cheese

1 lemon, juiced

½ cup heavy cream

½ teaspoon sea salt

3 tablespoons minced chives

1 Preheat oven to 325°. Lightly grease six soufflé cups (you can find disposable aluminum cups in the grocery store. Look for 10-ounce or 5-inch aluminum baking cups) with melted butter, using your pastry brush. Set the cups aside. Place your 1-quart saucepot over high heat and fill it most of the way up with water. Finely mince the shrimp and scallops together, until they are almost completely pulverized and turned into a paste. Add this seafood paste to a medium bowl.

2 Add the whole egg, egg yolk, ricotta, lemon juice, heavy cream, salt, and chives to the bowl of seafood. Fold together until evenly mixed. Divide the mixture amongst the six dishes and cover each one with a piece of foil.

3 Arrange the covered cups in a 9 x 13-inch baking dish , and place it on the middle rack of the oven. Carefully pull the rack out a few inches, and pour the hot water that has been heating in your saucepan into the bottom of the baking dish until it reaches halfway up the side of the cups.

4 Bake the timbales for 35 minutes, and then use your tongs to carefully remove one cup from the baking dish. You'll really look like a gourmet chef when you do this! Carefully lift off the foil, and, if the timbale has shrunk from the sides and is firm to the touch, it is done. If the timbale has not set, return it to the oven and bake for another 5 minutes or until firm. Remove the entire pan from the oven, uncover each cup, and allow them to cool slightly. Drain away any liquid that has formed around the timbale, and then turn them out onto a clean plate. To serve as a single course, place the timbale in the center of a salad plate and top with two tablespoons of They Call Me Mellow Yellow Sauce (p. 190), allowing the sauce to drizzle down the sides.

Kick-Your-Caboose Saffron Couscous

Serves 4 to 6

Couscous can be made in a matter of minutes and only requires one pot, making it exceptionally CLK friendly.

- 1¾ cups vegetable or chicken stock
- 1 teaspoon sea salt
- ½ orange, juiced
- 6 saffron threads
- 1½ cups couscous
- 4 tablespoons unsalted butter
- 2 tablespoons chopped fresh parsley
- ¼ cup natural sliced almonds, toasted

1 Put your 1-quart saucepot over medium heat and add the stock, sea salt, and freshly squeezed orange juice. When the liquid is hot and has begun to steam, add the saffron threads, allowing them to "bloom" or dissolve into the stock.

2 Once the water begins to simmer, add the couscous and the butter; cover, and remove from heat. Allow this to stand for 10 minutes, and then open the lid and fluff the couscous with a fork.

3 Taste the couscous at this point to see if it needs more salt, then stir in the parsley. For a restaurant style plating, take a small can (like a tuna can) and wash it thoroughly. Line it with plastic wrap (in case the couscous doesn't want to release), and then pack the can very tightly with the couscous. Turn over and tap lightly in the center of the plate. A perfect cylinder of golden couscous should be left behind. Garnish with the toasted almonds.

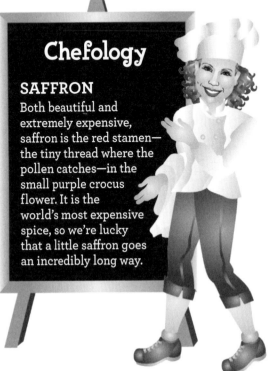

Chefology

SAFFRON

Both beautiful and extremely expensive, saffron is the red stamen—the tiny thread where the pollen catches—in the small purple crocus flower. It is the world's most expensive spice, so we're lucky that a little saffron goes an incredibly long way.

Saucy Sauces

It has been said that the British have three sauces and 360 religions, whereas the French have three religions and 360 sauces. The number of religions aside, five "mother sauces" serve as the basis for the hundreds of sauces that can be developed. They are espagnole, béchamel, velouté, hollandaise, and tomato. I've covered all of them in one form or another in this chapter. Regardless of the state of your Crappy Little Kitchen, with a little practice you will attain new heights as an accomplished CLK chef with your ability to create and master these magnificent sauces.

Not only are sauces the cornerstone of delectable gourmet meals, but they also qualify as genuine one-pot wonders!

They Call Me Mellow Yellow Sauce

Yields 1½ cups

This sauce pairs beautifully with absolutely any seafood including mussels, scallops, white fish, or lobster but will also marry well with any number of grains such as couscous, quinoa, or pasta.

4 threads saffron

¾ cup chicken stock, warm

1 tablespoon unsalted butter

2 teaspoons all-purpose flour

½ cup heavy cream

Sea salt, to taste

Black pepper, to taste

1 tablespoon finely chopped chives

1 First, add the saffron threads to the chicken stock, allowing the saffron to "bloom" or dissolve into the stock. Put your 1-quart saucepot over medium heat and melt the butter. Once it has become foamy, add the flour and stir constantly while the light roux cooks for 3 minutes.

2 Gradually stir in the saffron infused stock until it forms brilliant gravy, and then drizzle in the heavy cream. When fully combined, turn the heat down to low, and season with salt and freshly cracked pepper. Taste to see if it needs more seasoning, and stir in the chopped chives. Serve warm.

Gorgonzola and Walnut Sauce

 Yields
2½ cups

This sauce is perfect for pastas and grilled flank steak, and it is delicious drizzled over the Herb Crusted Pork Tenderloin (p. 118).

4 tablespoons unsalted butter

½ cup roughly chopped walnut pieces

½ cup vegetable stock

½ cup heavy cream

4 ounces gorgonzola cheese

½ cup grated pecorino cheese

2 tablespoons honey

Sea salt, to taste

Black pepper, freshly cracked, to taste

1 Melt the butter in your 1-quart sauce pot over medium heat, and add the walnut pieces. Toast the walnuts in the butter for 15 minutes, stirring occasionally.

2 Add the vegetable stock and heavy cream, and raise the temperature slightly, bringing the mixture to a simmer. Simmer slowly for 3 to 5 minutes, and then stir in the gorgonzola, pecorino, and honey.

3 Gorgonzola cheeses will vary in salty flavor, so be sure to taste the sauce before you season it with sea salt and freshly cracked pepper. Serve warm.

Low-Maintenance Lemon Tarragon Sauce

Yields 3¼ cups

One of the chefs I used to work for always sings the praises of tarragon cream sauce with chicken and pasta. Try it, and you'll agree. This sauce requires very little chopping and therefore, very few crappy dirty dishes. I think the addition of lemon gives the flavor profile a blast of sunshine that is well deserved.

3 tablespoons unsalted butter

3 tablespoons all-purpose flour

2½ cups chicken stock

¼ cup half-and-half

Sea salt, to taste

1 lemon, zested and juiced

3 tablespoons chopped fresh tarragon leaves

2 tablespoons extra virgin olive oil

1 shallot, finely chopped

¼ cup dry white wine

3 tablespoons heavy cream

2 tablespoons brandy

Black pepper, to taste

1 Heat your 1-quart saucepot over medium heat, and melt the butter. Once it has become foamy, add the flour and stir constantly while the light roux cooks for 1 minute. Gradually stir in the stock until it forms a thick sauce, and then drizzle in the half-and-half. Season the sauce at this point to taste with sea salt, and then leave it on low heat. This is called a velouté sauce and will be added later.

Swap It

Make the Superlative Stuffed Chicken Breast (p. 117), eliminating the sage so it doesn't compete with the tarragon, and then pour this sauce over the top for a delightful combination. Toss it through pasta or drizzle over the crispy I'm a Softy for Soft-Shell Crab (p.110) to reinvent these recipes.

2 Combine the lemon zest with the chopped tarragon, and set them aside. Heat your 8-quart stockpot over medium heat and add the olive oil. Add the chopped shallot to the heated olive oil, season lightly with salt, and allow it to soften for 3 minutes. When it becomes translucent, add the white wine and simmer until it has reduced by half.

3 Stir in the lemon zest and tarragon, the lemon juice, and gradually drizzle in the Velouté. Add the cream and brandy. Turn the heat down to low and allow the sauce to infuse with the tarragon and lemon for about 3 minutes. Season to taste with salt and freshly cracked black pepper. Serve warm.

Apple Cider Beurre Blanc

Yields 2 cups

The very first Christmas dinner I hosted in my home included this sauce served over seared duck breast. A true beurre blanc would not have cream as an ingredient, but this addition makes the sauce more stable (meaning less likely to curdle), and therefore CLK friendly. An incredibly rich sauce, it is best paired with something mild yet able to stand up to the velvety sauce, such as the Hunka Hunka Monkfish (p. 104).

½ cup apple cider

½ cup apple cider vinegar

½ cup dry white wine

2 shallots, sliced

1 garlic clove, smashed

6 black peppercorns

½ cup heavy cream

1 pound unsalted butter

Sea salt, to taste

1 Place your 1-quart saucepot over medium-high heat and add the cider, vinegar, and wine. Allow the liquid to simmer and add the shallot, garlic, and peppercorns. This should simmer away for 10 to 15 minutes as it reduces to a syrup. Once it has reduced to a few table-spoons of liquid, whisk in the heavy cream. Lower the heat to medium, and continue reducing for 10 more minutes. Once large bubbles begin to form, the cream has also thickened to syrup.

2 Lower your heat again to medium-low, and begin whisking the reduction to disperse some of the heat. Drop in 1 tablespoon of butter at a time, whisking to integrate each pad of butter into the sauce; don't add the next tablespoon of butter until the last is completely incorporated. As you continue to add butter, piece by piece, you'll notice the sauce begin to emulsify and the color will lighten slightly. Once all the butter is incorporated, remove it from the heat.

3 Season to taste with sea salt, and run it through your strainer to remove the shallot, garlic, and peppercorns. If you need to keep it warm for a significant amount of time before you serve it, heat 2 cups of water in a small saucepot over low heat, pour the sauce into a heat resistant bowl, and place the bowl over the warm water. Turn the burner off and stir occasionally. If you leave the beurre blanc on direct heat, the butter will separate from the sauce, which would be crappy.

Easy Cheesy Cheddar and Fontina Sauce

Yields 6 cups

This sauce guarantees kids will enjoy their broccoli or Brussels sprouts, and will help adults rediscover macaroni and cheese. Pour it on steamed vegetables or stir it into cooked pasta. Easy cheesy! Everyone loves it.

3 tablespoons unsalted butter

3 tablespoons all-purpose flour

2 cups whole milk

1 bay leaf, fresh

2 cups shredded aged Cheddar cheese

2 cups shredded Fontina cheese

1 pinch ground nutmeg

Sea salt, to taste

Black pepper, freshly ground, to taste

1 Melt the butter in your 12-quart saucepot over medium heat. Whisk the flour into the melted butter and allow it to cook slowly for 8 minutes, whisking occasionally. Slowly drizzle in the milk while whisking constantly to keep the sauce from becoming lumpy, and add the bay leaf. Allow this mixture to simmer, whisking often, until it becomes thick and smooth, about 10 minutes.

2 Remove from the heat and stir in the Cheddar, Fontina, and nutmeg. Stir until the cheese is melted, and strain to remove the bay leaf and any lumps. Use a heat resistant spatula to push the sauce through your strainer if it needs any help, but this step will make your sauce velvety smooth. Season to taste with sea salt and plenty of freshly cracked black pepper. Serve warm.

Béarnaise Sauce

Yields
1 cup

A very traditional herb butter sauce, béarnaise brilliantly allows meat and vegetables to stand out while simply adding a hint of sophistication. This sauce whisks to fluffy perfection in 5 minutes. It's even delicious on French fries!

3 tablespoons white wine vinegar

2 tablespoons water

1 shallot, minced

¼ cup fresh tarragon leaves

6 black peppercorns

2 egg yolks

½ cup unsalted butter, cubed

1 teaspoon chopped fresh tarragon

1 teaspoon chopped fresh parsley

1 teaspoon chopped fresh chervil

Sea salt, to taste

Ground white pepper, to taste

1 pinch cayenne pepper

1 Place your 1-quart saucepot over medium to high heat and add the vinegar, water, shallot, tarragon, and black peppercorns. Bring to a simmer and reduce the liquid by half. Strain out all of the solids and allow your reduced vinegar to cool slightly.

2 While this mixture is cooling, add about 1½ cups of water back into the 1-quart saucepot and put it over medium heat. In a medium bowl, whisk the egg yolks while slowly drizzling in the vinegar. Put the bowl over the pot of water and continue whisking while the mixture becomes light and fluffy. If the water begins to boil, turn down the heat; you only want a light simmer.

3 Slowly whisk in the butter, one cube at a time, continuously whisking until each cube is completely incorporated. Whisk in the herbs and season to taste with salt, white pepper, and cayenne. Serve warm.

Finger-Licking Chipotle Aioli

Yields
1½ cups

This aioli will compliment any meat, but it is especially wonderful on thinly sliced venison in all its gamey glory.

2 pasteurized egg yolks

1 teaspoon white wine vinegar

3 tablespoons garlic, minced

1 cup extra virgin olive oil

2 tablespoons chipotle, minced

1 tablespoon adobo sauce

Sea salt, to taste

1 Place a medium size bowl on top of a damp dishtowel. (This will keep the bowl from rolling around while you whisk.) Put the egg yolks, vinegar, and garlic into the bowl and whisk to combine.

2 While whisking vigorously with one hand, slowly drizzle in the olive oil with the other hand. If you add the oil too quickly, it won't emulsify (blend) with the yolks—so add the oil slowly. When properly emulsified, the sauce should be thick like mayonnaise. If yours seems too thin, simply continue whisking and drizzling in more oil until it thickens.

3 Fold in the chipotle and adobo, and season to taste with salt.

Swap It

You can add many things besides chipotle to the basic aioli we make for this recipe (through step 2). Try adding horseradish, tarragon, or lemon and dill. Mix in capers, minced red onion, and lemon for a seafood topper vastly superior to your everyday tartar sauce. Buy the canned chipotle in adobo sauce. If you are in a real big hurry, add the garlic, chipotle, and salt to one cup of real mayonnaise.

Crappy Little Kitchens

Stinky Cheese Crab Sauce

Yields 3 cups

Everyone should try this quick and easy sauce on a juicy steak, and those with a true love of stinky cheese can omit the crab and use this sauce on anything! Or start with, My Personal Wellington recipe (p. 126), but stop at the end of step 1. Once the steak is crispy on all sides, allow it to rest for 5 minutes (to let the juices inside settle down so they don't come pouring out when your guest cuts into their steak), and pile the cheesy crab sauce on top. Alternatively, serve it with steamed vegetables (p. 168), drizzle it over your Seafood Risotto (p. 160), or put a bowl of it next to a crusty baguette for a delicious bread dip.

3 tablespoons unsalted butter

¼ cup very small diced yellow onion

1 garlic clove, mashed

Sea salt, to taste

3 tablespoons all-purpose flour

2 cups whole milk

1 fresh bay leaf or substitute 1 dry

8 ounces Taleggio cheese, rind removed

8 ounces select crab-meat

1 pinch cayenne pepper

1 Melt the butter in your 1-quart saucepot over medium heat. Add the onion and garlic clove, sautéing them until they become soft. Season lightly with salt. Whisk the flour into the melted butter and allow it to cook slowly for 8 minutes, whisking often. Slowly drizzle in the milk while whisking constantly to keep the sauce from being lumpy, and add the bay leaf. Allow this mixture to simmer, whisking often, until it becomes thick and smooth, about 10 minutes.

2 Remove from the heat and add the Taleggio and crab. Stir until the cheese is melted, and remove the bay leaf and garlic clove. Season to taste with sea salt and a pinch of cayenne. Serve warm.

Duck Hollandaise Sauce

Yields
1 cup This recipe calls for duck fat, which most specialty markets carry in the freezer section, but you can also order it from your butcher. Because the melted duck fat is pure golden fat, void of the milk solids present in melted butter, this hollandaise whisks up clean and easy.

2 tablespoons white
   wine vinegar

1 tablespoon water

6 black peppercorns

1 bay leaf

2 egg yolks

½ cup duck fat, melted
   in the microwave

Sea salt, to taste

Ground white pepper,
   to taste

1 pinch cayenne pepper

1 Place your 1-quart saucepot over medium to high heat and add the vinegar, water, peppercorns, and bay leaf. Bring to a simmer and reduce the liquid by half. Strain out all of the solids and allow your reduced vinegar to cool slightly.

2 While this mixture is cooling, add about 1½ cups of water back into the 1-quart saucepot and put it over low heat. In a medium bowl, whisk the egg yolks while slowly drizzling in the vinegar. Put the bowl over the pot of water and continue whisking. If the water begins to boil, turn down the heat; you only want a light simmer.

3 Slowly drizzle in the melted duck fat, continuously whisking until all the fat is completely incorporated. Season to taste with salt, white pepper, and cayenne. Serve warm with roasted potatoes or the Asparagus Salad (p. 92).

Champagne Velouté Sauce

Yields 2 cups

I paired this sauce with wild striped bass on one of my very first menus. I was so proud of the dish I served it to my father while he was entertaining business associates in my restaurant. Use a sparkling wine you enjoy drinking, because this recipe only needs two cups—you get to drink the rest!

2 cups Champagne

½ cup chicken broth

2 tablespoons unsalted butter

2 tablespoons all-purpose flour

2 tablespoons half-and-half

Sea salt, to taste

1 pinch nutmeg

1 pinch ground ginger

1 Place your 1-quart saucepot over high heat and add the Champagne and chicken broth. Simmer them together until the mixture has reduced slightly, about 8 minutes. Transfer the liquid to a heat-resistant container to hold for a few minutes.

Rinse the pot, put it back on medium heat and melt the butter. Whisk the flour into the melted butter and allow it to cook slowly for 8 minutes, whisking often. Slowly drizzle in the reduced Champagne while whisking constantly to keep the sauce from becoming lumpy. Then add the half-and-half. Allow this mixture to simmer, whisking often, until it becomes thick, yet light and creamy. Season to taste with sea salt, nutmeg, and ground ginger. Serve warm drizzled over any white meat, but especially white flaky fish.

Artichoke Mousseline Sauce

Yields
1 cup

The ingredient of whipped cream helps to stabilize this sauce, so you'll have no worries about messing it up! Pair it with the Snake-Charmin' Moroccan Lamb Chops (page 130), for a gourmet taste sensation.

2 egg yolks

1 lemon juiced

6 tablespoons unsalted butter

½ cup chopped canned artichoke hearts

6 tablespoons heavy cream

Sea salt, to taste

Ground white pepper, to taste

1 Add about 1½ cups of water into your 1-quart saucepot, and put it over medium heat. Place a medium bowl on top of the pot of water, and whisk the egg yolks while slowly drizzling in half of the lemon juice. Continue whisking vigorously until the mixture is very thick and fluffy. If the water begins to boil, turn down the heat; you only want a light simmer.

2 Slowly whisk in the butter, one cube at a time, continuously whisking until each

Swap It

Instead of artichokes, add chopped capers and use this sauce on the Champagne Oysters (p. 46). Try any number of ingredient combinations like adding dill to the lemony mousseline and serving it on artichoke hearts (Get Stoked for Artichokes p. 30), or rosemary and lemon mousseline on chicken breast.

Buttermilk Panna Cotta, p. 224

Coconut Poached Pears with Burgundy Sauce, p. 229

Citrus Peach Upside-Down Cake, p. 238

Heavenly Cheesecake, p. 246

cube is completely incorporated. Using a heat-resistant spatula, fold in the artichoke. Clean and dry your whisk and then in another bowl, whisk the heavy cream until it will stand up on the edge of your whisk. Using the spatula, carefully fold the whipped cream into the artichoke mixture.

3 Season the sauce to taste with the rest of the lemon juice, salt, and white pepper. Serve warm.

Chefology

MOUSSELINE (pronounced moos-LEEN) Any sauce that uses whipped cream or beaten eggs to give it a light and airy consistency.

Espagnole Sauce

Yields 3 cups

Espagnole, the classic French brown sauce, is perfect for any red meat, especially wild game. This recipe calls for veal stock, but feel free to substitute beef stock, particularly if you already have some in your crappy little pantry.

2 tablespoons unsalted butter

2 tablespoons vegetable oil

¼ cup finely chopped shallots

2 tablespoons finely chopped carrot

2 tablespoons finely chopped celery

1 tablespoon tomato paste

3 tablespoons all-purpose flour

3 cups veal or beef stock

1 thin white sock, new

2 parsley stems

2 thyme stems

1 garlic clove

½ teaspoon whole black peppercorns

1 fresh bay leaf, or substitute 1 dried

Sea salt, to taste

Black pepper, to taste

1 Place your 1-quart saucepot over medium to high heat, and add the butter and vegetable oil. When the butter has completely melted into the oil, add the shallot, carrot, and celery, stirring them once to allow them to coat with oil and butter. Now allow them to brown, by only stirring once every few minutes.

2 When the vegetables are a golden brown, turn the heat down to medium and add the tomato paste. Whisk constantly until all the tomato is evenly dispersed, and then do the same with the flour. Cook this roux for 8 minutes, stirring constantly until it turns a rich brown color.

3 While stirring vigorously, drizzle in the veal stock. Allow this to come up to a simmer. Put the parsley, thyme, garlic clove, black pepper, and bay leaf into the white sock, and tie the top tightly. This is called a sachet. Add it to the sauce.

4 Simmer for about 30 minutes and skim off any foam that forms. Remove and discard the sachet. Strain the sauce, and taste for salt or black pepper.

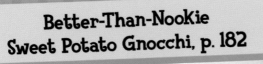
Better-Than-Nookie
Sweet Potato Gnocchi, p. 182

Call the Po-Po on This Polenta, p. 177

Classic Bolognese
Sauce, p. 213

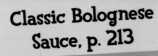

Duck Hollandaise Sauce, p. 200

Béarnaise Sauce, p. 197

Espagnole Sauce, p. 204

Charred Tomato
Red Wine Demi Sauce

Yields
4 cups Don't think it's a cop-out to buy prepared demi glace for this recipe.
A proper demi glace takes hours to cook to the right consistency at home.
Demi glace is available in the freezer section at specialty markets and makes this
recipe a cinch to prepare.

6 Roma tomatoes

3 tablespoons extra
virgin olive oil, plus
more for drizzling
on tomatoes

⅓ cup thinly sliced
shallots

3 garlic cloves,
sliced

3 thyme stems
(save the leaves
in the fridge for
another day)

Sea salt, to taste

Black pepper, to taste

1 cup big red wine
(Cabernet or
Zinfandel)

2 cups prepared
demi glace

1 Preheat oven to 400°. Cut the tomatoes in
half lengthwise, and place skin down on a
sheet tray. Drizzle the tomatoes with some olive
oil. Put the tray in the oven for 30 minutes or
until the tomatoes are mostly black. Remove the
tray from the oven and set it aside.

2 Place your 1-quart saucepot over medium
heat, and add 3 tablespoons of olive oil.
When the oil is hot, add the shallot, garlic, and
thyme. Season lightly with salt and pepper, and
sweat them to release all their juices. Add the
red wine and turn the heat to high, allowing it
to reduce to syrup, which should take about
5 to 10 minutes.. Once most of the liquid is
gone remove the thyme stems, and add the
demi glace.

3 Reduce the heat to medium and add all the
tomatoes along with their juices. Stir them
gently into the reduction until well combined,
which should take about 10 minutes.

4 Puree in your blender. Strain the mixture through your fine strainer, and
then season it to taste with salt and pepper.
Serve warm drizzled around the My Personal
Wellington (p. 126) or as a flavorful dipping
sauce for bruschetta (p. 28).

Mandarin Orange Sauce

Yields
3 cups Usually paired with roasted duck in my house, any wild or gamey bird would benefit from this sauce's sweet and tangy goodness. You don't have to worry about breaking this sauce if it gets too hot, so give it a try.

2 cups duck or chicken stock

⅔ cup red wine, preferably a Pinot Noir

1 shallot, thinly sliced

6 whole black peppercorns

8 fresh mandarin oranges, juice plus zest

1 tablespoon orange liqueur

½ cup red currant jelly

Sea salt, to taste

1 Place your 1-quart saucepot over high heat, and add stock, red wine, shallot, and peppercorns. Allow this mixture to simmer until it reduces by half, and then strain out the shallot and peppercorns, returning the liquid to the pot.

2 Add the juice and zest from the oranges and the orange liqueur to the reduction, and return the pot to the heat. Lower the heat to medium and stir in the currant jelly. When this comes to a simmer, remove it from the heat, and season to taste with salt. Serve warm with wild roasted birds such as quail or pheasant. You can also baste your Thanksgiving turkey or holiday goose with this sauce in the last 15 minutes of roasting to aide in the browning.

Pretty Peverada Sauce

Yields
4 cups

The ultimate fish sauce, peverada contains every element that any fish has ever cried out for: garlic, anchovy, pork, bread crumbs, parsley, lemon, and cheese. Peverada will stand up to a strong fish like tuna or salmon but will also amplify the mild flavor of fish like halibut or trout. My favorite pairs for this sauce are the intensely rich buttery monkfish or sea bass. Just like my crappy kitchen, a little bit of this goes a long way, so drizzle on just enough to coat the top of the fish.

1 cup olive oil

1½ tablespoon minced garlic

4 anchovy fillets, minced

1⅓ cup minced hard salami, about 6 ounces

¼ cup plain bread crumbs

½ cup Italian parsley

¼ cup lemon zest

1⅓ cup vegetable stock

¼ cup fresh lemon juice

¼ cup freshly grated Parmesan cheese

Sea salt, to taste

Black pepper, to taste

1 Place your 1-quart saucepot over medium heat and add the olive oil and garlic, cooking until softened. Add the anchovy, salami, bread crumbs, parsley, and lemon zest. Cook 2 minutes. Add the vegetable stock and reduce slightly.

2 Remove the pot from the heat and finish the sauce by adding the lemon juice and Parmesan cheese. Taste the sauce because it won't need much salt, but it will certainly need some black pepper. Serve warm.

Citrus Beurre Blanc Sauce

Yields 1 cup

A traditional beurre blanc sauce is a classic French white sauce made from an acidic reduction and butter. This rendition goes especially well with freshly blanched spring and summer vegetables or as an additional sauce for the Barbequeless Barbequed Salmon (p. 106).

½ cup pineapple juice

½ cup lemon juice

½ cup dry white wine

2 shallots, sliced

1 garlic clove, smashed

¼ cup heavy cream

1 pound unsalted butter

Sea salt, to taste

White pepper, to taste

1 Place your 1-quart saucepot over medium-high heat and add the pineapple juice, lemon juice, and wine. Allow the liquid to simmer and add the shallot and garlic. Let this simmer for 10 to 15 minutes as it reduces to syrup. When only a few tablespoons of liquid remain, whisk in the heavy cream, lower the heat to medium, and continue reducing for 10 more minutes until large bubbles form, at which point the cream has become a syrup.

2 Lower the heat again to medium-low, and begin slowly whisking the reduction to disperse some of the heat. Drop in 1 tablespoon of butter at a time, whisking to integrate each pad of butter; and don't add the next tablespoon of butter until the last is completely incorporated. As you continue to add butter, piece by piece, you'll notice the sauce begin to emulsify and the color will lighten slightly. Once all the butter is incorporated, remove it from the heat.

3 Run it through your strainer to remove the shallot and garlic. Use a heat resistant spatula to push the sauce through your strainer if it needs any help, as this step will make your sauce velvety smooth. Season to taste with sea salt and white pepper. If you need to keep the sauce warm for a significant amount of time before you serve dinner, heat 2 cups of water in a small saucepot over low heat, pour the sauce into a heat resistant bowl, and place the bowl over the warm water. Turn off the burner, and stir occasionally. Serve warm.

Swap It

I like to keep this sauce balanced with the sweetness of pineapple juice and the sourness of bright lemon. Feel free to experiment with other citrus fruits by using orange and grapefruit or lemon and lime.

Mighty Marinara Sauce

**Yields
3 cups**

A truly traditional marinara is made with fresh Roma tomatoes at the peak of their season, with the addition of only garlic, sea salt, and maybe fresh herbs. Because juicy ripe tomatoes aren't always available, I make mine with canned plum tomatoes, which are sealed at the height of freshness in their own juices. This recipe makes a wonderful gourmet pasta sauce, and all you need is one crappy pot!

¼ cup extra virgin
   olive oil

3 shallots, minced

5 garlic cloves, minced

35 ounces crushed
   plum tomatoes,
   canned

Sea salt, to taste

Black pepper, to taste

Red pepper flakes,
   to taste

3 tablespoons finely
   chopped thyme
   leaves

3 tablespoons finely
   chopped oregano

1 Place your 12-quart stockpot over medium heat and add the olive oil. Add the shallot and garlic, cooking until softened and lightly browned.

2 Add the can of tomatoes and allow it to come to a boil. Season the sauce to taste with salt, black pepper, and red pepper flakes. Lower the heat to low and allow it to cook slowly for 45 minutes. Add the herbs and cook another 5 minutes. Serve warm tossed through or slathered over No-Space Meatballs (p. 34) as an entrée or even as a beautiful warm sandwich.

210

Crappy Little Kitchens

Spicy Pomodoro Sauce

Yields
3 cups
This utilitarian sauce holds together sheets of lasagna, vegetables, and cheese or serves as the perfect topper for pizza crust. It's quick and easy to make but tastes as though it took all day. Try it as a quick sauce paired with a more labor-intensive dish such as Fried Green Tomatoes (p. 38) or homemade pasta, or whip it up if you're just in a hurry.

3 tablespoons extra
virgin olive oil

½ cup chopped shallots

4 garlic cloves,
crushed

35 ounces crushed
plum tomatoes,
canned

2 teaspoons red
pepper flake

10 fresh basil leaves,
chopped

Sea salt, to taste

Black pepper, to taste

1 Place your 12-quart stockpot over medium heat and add the olive oil. Add the shallots and garlic, cooking until softened and lightly browned.

2 Add the can of tomatoes, allowing it to come to a boil. Sprinkle in the red pepper flakes, lower the heat to low, and allow it to cook slowly for 20 minutes, stirring often. Add the basil and remove from the heat.

3 Pour the mixture into your blender, and puree the sauce. Season to taste with salt and pepper. Serve warm.

I'm a Maniac for Mexican Mole Sauce

Yields
4 cups A spicy Mexican sauce, mole usually contains onion, chilies, nuts or seeds, and unsweetened chocolate and is served with meat or poultry. In this recipe, fresh tomato provides color as well as an appealing texture to the sauce, while the chocolate smoothes out any bitterness from the dried chiles and brings depth to the flavor.

¼ cup olive oil

½ cup chopped shallot

4 garlic cloves

½ cup blanched
   almonds, toasted

4 cups vegetable stock

2 ancho chilies

2 guajillo chilies

4 Roma tomatoes

½ banana

1 cinnamon stick

4 whole cloves

1 ounce Mexican
   chocolate, chopped

Sea salt, to taste

Black pepper, to taste

1 In your 12-quart stockpot, heat the olive oil over medium heat, and add the shallots, garlic, and almonds. When the shallots have begun to brown, pour the mixture into your blender. Rinse the pot, and return it to the heat and add the vegetable stock.

2 Add the chilies to the stock and simmer until soft, about 15 minutes. Pour the stock, along with the chiles, into the blender with the shallots, garlic, and almonds. Gently pulse the entire mixture until pureed, then use your strainer to strain the sauce back into the sauce-pot, and use a heat resistant spatula to push the sauce through your strainer if it needs any help. Place over low heat. Add the tomatoes, banana, cinnamon stick, and cloves to the saucepot, and simmer for 1 hour, stirring frequently. Pour into your blender, pulse gently until smooth, and then strain one last time, just as before.

3 Add the chocolate and stir until melted. Season to taste with salt and pepper. Serve with your Mushroom Tamales (p. 138), or make traditional chicken mole by simmering chicken quarters (legs, thighs, and breast still on the bone) in the finished sauce.

Classic Bolognese Sauce

Yields
6 cups

The gourmet trick in this recipe is to use tomato puree instead of crushed tomatoes. The puree not only increases the richness but it also allows the meat to take center stage in the sauce. Try it tossed with fresh pasta first, and then, once you've seen the possibilities, use it tossed with steamed mussels or as the meat sauce for lasagna. Feel free to make a double batch and freeze half into 3-quart-size freezer bags. Lay the bags flat in your freezer to save space and for easy defrosting for Bolognese on demand in your Crappy Little Kitchen. Just pull a bag out of the freezer the night before you'd like to serve it, and the next day it should be thawed enough to be reheated inside a saucepot.

3 tablespoons extra virgin olive oil

2 cups small diced Pancetta about 12 ounces

1 cup minced yellow onion

½ cup minced carrot

½ cup minced celery

3 tablespoons minced garlic

1 pound ground veal

1 pound ground pork

½ cup dry red wine

2 fresh bay leaves, or substitute 1 dried

28 ounces beef stock or broth

15 ounces tomato puree, canned

1 cup whole milk

1 tablespoon chopped fresh thyme

Sea salt, to taste

Black pepper, to taste

Parmigiano-Reggiano cheese, as needed

1 Place your 12-quart stockpot over medium-high heat and add the olive oil. Add the pancetta and sauté until it begins to brown, about 6 minutes. Add the onion, carrot, celery, and garlic, sautéing for 5 minutes, stirring occasionally. Add the veal and pork, breaking up the meat with the back of a fork. Sauté until brown and cooked through. This should take another 10 minutes.

2 Pour in the wine and add the bay leaves. Simmer for about 10 minutes until the liquid is slightly reduced. Stir in the stock and tomato puree.

3 Reduce heat to medium-low and simmer, stirring often, until sauce thickens, about 1 hour and 15 minutes. Stir in the whole milk, and season with the fresh thyme, salt, and pepper. Serve warm with Parmesan cheese grated over the top.

Power-Play Portuguese Sauce

Yields
4 cups This is the recipe to help you realize the power of sauce. A very simple formula with such modest ingredients, yet the result is far too commanding for simple pasta. Add two dozen well scrubbed little neck clams after the tomatoes in step 2 and have a port-of-call gourmet experience like no other Crappy Little Kitchen has ever seen!

3 tablespoons extra
   virgin olive oil

1 yellow onion,
   small dice

8 ounces ground
   chorizo sausage

8 ounces ground pork

30 ounces crushed
   tomatoes, canned

1 cup dry white wine

½ teaspoon red pepper
   flakes

¼ cup chopped fresh
   cilantro (save pinch
   for garnish)

Sea salt, to taste

Black pepper, to taste

1   Heat your 12-inch sauté pan over medium-high heat and add the olive oil. Add the onion and allow it to soften. Stir until it's translucent. Add the chorizo and ground pork browning the meat well; this should take about 10 minutes.

2   Stir in the tomatoes and reduce the heat to medium. Allow the tomatoes to cook down for about 5 minutes, and then add the white wine, red pepper flakes, and chopped cilantro. Reduce this mixture slowly for 10 to 15 minutes.

3   Taste your sauce at this point and season to taste with salt and pepper. Garnish with the extra cilantro.

Pico de Gallo Salsa

This basic salsa recipe is excellent served with tortilla chips, as a garnish for Fried Green Tomatoes (p. 38), or topping the Chili Rellenos (p. 134).

2 large ripe tomatoes, medium dice

1 red onion, medium dice

½ teaspoon minced garlic

1 small jalapeno pepper, seeded, minced

2 tablespoons chopped fresh cilantro

3 tablespoons fresh lime juice

Sea salt, to taste

Black pepper, to taste

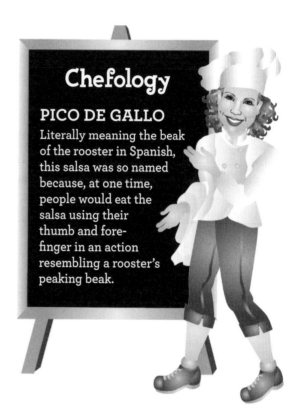

Chefology

PICO DE GALLO

Literally meaning the beak of the rooster in Spanish, this salsa was so named because, at one time, people would eat the salsa using their thumb and fore-finger in an action resembling a rooster's peaking beak.

Swap It

Play with the flavor of this versatile salsa by adding diced avocado or corn and black beans. You can dress up the salsa for guests by blackening your vegetables then pureeing them to create a charred version.

1 In a medium bowl, combine the tomato, onion, garlic, jalapeno, cilantro, and lime juice. Toss gently to combine evenly, and season to taste with salt and pepper.

2 Wrap tightly and refrigerate until ready to serve from a margarita glass in the center of a giant platter of nachos.

Sausage and Peppers Sauce

Yields 4 cups

This recipe is delicious tossed together with light egg pasta. If you want to make the sandwich version of sausage and peppers, omit the cream from the sauce, leave the sausage links whole, place them in toasted sub rolls, and slather the sauced peppers over the top.

3 tablespoons extra virgin olive oil

2 red bell peppers

2 green bell peppers

1 pound sweet Italian sausage

2 tablespoons unsalted butter

1 cup sliced yellow onion

2 cloves garlic, minced

¼ cup heavy cream

2 tablespoons chopped fresh oregano

Sea salt, to taste

Black pepper, to taste

1 Preheat your oven to 500°. Place the bell peppers on a sheet tray, and drizzle olive oil over them. Roast them in the oven for 15 to 20 minutes or until they begin to blacken and blister all over. Remove them with your tongs, and place them in a mixing bowl. Cover the bowl with plastic wrap, and let them rest as they steam and cool.

2 While waiting for the peppers to cool, heat your 12-inch sauté pan over medium-high heat. Place the sausage links into the hot pan. Sear the links on all sides until very brown, and then remove them to cool on your cutting board.

3 Put the butter, onion, and garlic in the same pan. Reduce the heat to medium. Allow the onion and garlic to cook until the onions are golden brown. Add the cream and oregano. Turn the heat down to medium low, and allow the sauce to reduce.

4 Now that the peppers are cool, pull off their tops and dump out the seeds and juice. Use your hands to peel off their charred skins, and then slice them into thick strips. Cut the sausage links into ¼-inch thick discs and add the sausage and peppers to the sauce.

5 Toss everything together and season to taste with salt and pepper. Serve warm.

Latin Salsa Verde

Yields
3 cups

This delicious Mexican green salsa is tangy, yet mild with tons of flavor. A great match for steak, fish, or chicken—think of it as the Mexican counterpart to ketchup. It's the perfect condiment to add dimension to almost any dish.

3 tablespoons olive oil

1 pound tomatillos

½ cup roughly chopped yellow onion

1 small jalapeno

2 garlic cloves

1 cup chicken stock

Sea salt, to taste

Black pepper, to taste

1 To easily remove their papery outer skins, put the tomatillos into a large bowl and cover them with warm water for about 10 minutes. Peel off the skins, and wash and dry the tomatillos.

2 Place your 12-inch sauté pan over medium heat and add the olive oil. When it begins to smoke, add the tomatilloes, onion, jalapeno, and garlic. Once the tomatillos begin to brown on one side, use your tongs to turn them over to brown on the other side. Wait one minute and add the chicken stock. Allow this to come to a simmer and bubble away for about 10 minutes.

3 Take the pan off the heat and allow it to cool for several minutes. Once it has cooled down, pour half of the mixture into your blender and gently pulse until smooth. Pour it into an airtight container, and repeat with the remaining tomatillo mixture.

4 Season to taste with salt and pepper. It's best served warm as a garnish for Not-So-Basic Black Bean Soup (p. 69) or as an additional sauce with Mushroom Tamales (p. 138).

Chefology

TOMATILLOS

Tomatillos have a papery outer skin and are used while they are still green. Although they are members of the tomato family, they are very tart and taste nothing like a tomato. If you can't find tomatillos you can substitute green tomatoes, but you'll need to add lemon juice for tartness.

Swanky Strawberry Salsa

Yields
2½ cups

Fruit salsas have become somewhat of a trend on contemporary menus these days, so feel free to add any fruit that you feel is salsa worthy. I love the bright color of strawberry salsa, but go ahead and try mango, pineapple, kiwi, or whatever you love that's in season. White flakey fish, like trout or Kona really benefit from a fresh salsa, as does green summer salads and the spicy Not-for-Chickens Chicken Soup (p. 62).

1 pound fresh
strawberries,
medium dice

½ red onion,
medium dice

1 Serrano pepper,
seeded and minced

1 tablespoon chopped
fresh parsley

2 tablespoons fresh
lime juice

½ teaspoon sugar

Sea salt, to taste

Black pepper, to taste

1 In a medium bowl, combine the strawberries, onion, Serrano pepper, parsley, lime juice, and sugar. Toss gently to combine evenly, and season to taste with salt and pepper.

2 Wrap tightly and refrigerate until chilled and ready to serve.

Booming Basil Pesto

Yield
1 cup

Pesto comes from the Italian word pestato, which means pounded. The ingredients for pesto are traditionally "pounded" together with a mortar and pestle. Today, we can mix the basil, pine nuts, and garlic effortlessly with a blender, while stirring the cheese in at the end for an ideal consistency.

1 cup firmly packed basil leaves

1 clove garlic

1 tablespoon pine nuts

3 tablespoons extra virgin olive oil

3 tablespoons freshly grated Parmigiano-Reggiano

Sea salt, to taste

Black pepper, to taste

1 In your blender, combine the basil, garlic, and pine nuts. Pulse a few times to make a basil paste. While blending on low (be ready, it may splash a bit), drizzle in your olive oil, and puree until smooth.

2 Stir in (do not blend or your pesto will be gummy) the parmesan cheese, and season with salt and pepper to taste.

Swap It

You can substitute one cup fresh spinach for the basil leaves to create a mild pesto alternative.

Desserts to Die For

What sets your Crappy Little Kitchen apart from

all the others, is the gourmet chef—you. When it comes to being a true chef, you must try to master all aspects of cooking, including preparing dessert. If you can make magnificent shrimp bisque or earth-shattering goat cheese soufflés you want your dessert to wow your guests as well.

Dessert can involve producing a complicated pastry or simply serving fresh berries with cream. Sometimes it may include baking, and other times you won't have to turn on the stove.

Strategically chosen for easy completion in your Crappy Little Kitchen, these dessert recipes stand out in taste as well as ease of preparation.

Desserts might consist of sugar and cinnamon or a savory cheese. As with all gourmet recipes, seasonal ingredients are integral to successful dessert making. In the CLK this is especially important because of the simplicity of my desserts. Strategically chosen for easy completion in your Crappy Little Kitchen, these dessert recipes stand out in taste as well as ease of preparation.

You'll learn how to present the desserts in an eye-pleasing fashion, but feel free to experiment. Try creating different dessert shapes (cut the cake slices into diamonds, for example), unique presentations (lean the lady fingers up against the mousse rather than stacking them on top), and using a variety of colors (fruits and berries come in a wide array of colors to choose from) until you find a style that suits and pleases you.

Buttermilk Panna Cotta

Serves 4

Light and creamy, this recipe represents a definitive gourmet summer dessert. It cooks in one pot and then chills in the fridge. You never have to turn on your crappy oven!

½ cup whole milk

2 teaspoons unflavored gelatin

½ cup sugar

1 tablespoon lemon juice

2 cups buttermilk

1 pinch sea salt

1 pint fresh berries

1   Add the milk to your 1-quart saucepot, and sprinkle in the gelatin. Allow this to sit for 5 minutes to soften the gelatin. Put this mixture over medium heat, and whisk in the sugar. Stir constantly until the sugar is dissolved.

Swap It

With a variation perfect for every season, cream desserts are just as versatile as they are delicious. Use the same basic custard recipe (either for panna cotta or crème brulee) while exchanging accompaniments to create a whole new gourmet dessert. Garnish the panna cotta with blood orange segments in the winter, add bing cherries to the bread pudding in the spring, and burn thinly sliced apple into the top of a brulee in the fall. Let the seasons and contents of your crappy little fridge dictate your inspirations.

2 Add the lemon, buttermilk, and pinch of salt, whisk to combine, and take it off the heat. Carefully strain the mixture into a large measuring cup. Pour this into 4 soufflé or coffee cups, cover them with small squares of plastic wrap, and set them on a level shelf in the refrigerator to chill.

3 After a minimum of 4 hours (preferably overnight), run your paring knife around each panna cotta and invert each dish over a small dessert plate. Scatter plenty of fresh berries on top of the panna cotta as well as around the plate, and serve immediately.

Chefology

PANNA COTTA

Panna Cotta means "cooked cream" in Italian, and it is no wonder why. This silky-smooth Italian pudding compliments any fresh fruit or berry in season. The perfect dinner party dessert, panna cotta is best when made a day or two in advance.

Bread Pudding with Bourbon Crème Anglaise

No fall or winter family gathering would be complete without this rich and classic dessert.

2 one-pound loaves brioche

½ cup dried cherries

½ cup golden raisins

1 cup Kentucky bourbon

¼ cup pecan pieces, toasted

1 cup whole milk

1 cup heavy cream

1 vanilla bean, scraped

4 egg yolks

¼ cup sugar

Sugar in the raw, as needed

1 Preheat the oven to 350°. Slice your brioche into ¼-inch slices, and lay them out on sheet trays to toast in the oven for 15 minutes. While it toasts, cover the cherries and raisins with the bourbon for 15 minutes. Strain them and reserve the bourbon.

2 Make 1 layer of toasted brioche in a 9 x 13-inch baking dish, and sprinkle with a few of the cherries, raisins, and toasted pecans. Continue layering like this until you run out of bread. Use any leftover fruit or nuts to garnish the finished dessert.

Swap It

Instead of bourbon, feel free to use your favorite whisky or even rum to customize the sauce to your liking. Try layering sliced apple, pitted fresh cherries, or ripe bananas in between the layers of bread as variations on traditional bread pudding. If you can't find brioche, Challah or even cinnamon raisin bread are perfect substitutes, but any crappy bread is better than having no bread pudding at all! Even leftover biscuits or muffins from breakfast work well.

How to Remove the Seeds from Vanilla Beans

Use your chef's knife to cut a vanilla bean lengthwise from end to end. Scrape the inside of the bean with the edge of your knife to remove the tiny black seeds inside.

3 Add the milk, heavy cream, and vanilla bean to your 1-quart saucepot. Put this over medium to low heat and wait for it to simmer.

4 In a large mixing bowl, whisk together the egg yolks and sugar. Then set the bowl on top of a damp towel to secure it and free up both of your hands. When the milk begins to simmer and rise up the sides of the pot, slowly drizzle it into the bowl of sugar and eggs while you whisk it vigorously. If you pour the scalded milk in too quickly or don't mix your eggs while pouring, it could overheat and scramble the eggs, which would be crappy.

5 Evenly pour all but ¼ cup of the custard over the dish of toasted brioche layers. Place another 9 x 13-inch baking dish (disposable is fine, but you'll want to fill it ¼ of the way up with dried beans to create weight) over the bread and custard to help weigh it down, and place the whole thing in the oven. While this bakes for 45 minutes, add 2 tablespoons of bourbon into the reserved custard, making your bourbon crème anglaise.

6 After 45 minutes, remove the weight from the pan, sprinkle the raw sugar over the bread pudding, and continue baking for 15 minutes, allowing the top to brown. Once the pudding is golden brown, remove it from the oven and cool for 10 minutes. Serve warm slices with a drizzle of the bourbon anglaise and a sprinkle of cherries, raisins, and pecans.

Did You Know This Crap?

Raw sugar provides an appetizing, pastry-shop finish to baked desserts. Despite the name, raw sugar is processed, however unlike white sugar, which has had the molasses (a by-product of refining) removed during processing, raw sugar contains a bit of the molasses residue, which provides its earthy color and round flavor.

Butterscotch Crème Brulee

Serves
6

I love bananas or fresh strawberries with this custard, but use whatever fruit looks freshest or that you enjoy the most.

1½ cups whole milk

1½ cups heavy cream

1 vanilla bean, scraped

8 egg yolks

½ cup brown sugar

3 tablespoons dark
   molasses

3 tablespoons Scotch

1 pinch sea salt

1 banana, thinly sliced

Sugar in the raw,
   as needed

1 Preheat the oven to 350°. In your 1-quart saucepot, add the milk, heavy cream, and vanilla bean. Put this over medium to low heat and wait for it to simmer.

2 In a large mixing bowl, whisk together the egg yolks, brown sugar, molasses, Scotch, and sea salt. When the milk begins to simmer and rise up the sides of the pot, slowly drizzle it into the bowl of sugar and eggs while you whisk it vigorously.

3 Carefully pour the incorporated mixture into a large measuring cup. Place 6 soufflé or coffee cups in a large baking dish and add hot tap water until it reaches ½ way up the sides of the cups. Fill the cups ¾ full with the brulee mixture, and place the entire baking dish into the oven.

4 Bake for 45 minutes to an hour, or until the custard has set (when jiggled gently the custard should not wiggle). Carefully use your tongs to remove the cups from the hot water, and place them in the refrigerator to chill. After the custard has cooled (about an hour), arrange a single layer of sliced bananas over each brulee, then sprinkle on a thin layer of raw sugar. Fire up your torch, keeping the flame about 2 inches from the banana slices, and melt the sugar.

Crappy Little Kitchens

Coconut Poached Pears with Burgundy Sauce

Serves 8

Crisp and juicy fall pears, a vibrant color combination, and ease in preparation make this dessert a chic addition to an autumn dinner party.

2 cups burgundy wine

1 cinnamon stick

⅓ cup plus 2 tablespoons sugar

2 cups coconut milk

1 vanilla bean, scraped

4 ripe pears, peeled with stem attached

4 fresh mint sprigs

1 In your 1-quart saucepot, add the wine, cinnamon stick, and 2 tablespoons of sugar. Place this over high heat, and stir until the sugar has dissolved. Allow this to come to a boil and cook until reduced by half.

2 Place your 12-inch sauté pan over medium heat and add your coconut milk, vanilla bean, and ⅓ cup of sugar. Stir until the sugar is dissolved. Allow it to come to a simmer, but watch it carefully to properly regulate the temperature so it doesn't boil or it will separate. Cut each of the pears in half vertically straight through the stem, leaving the stems halves intact. Scoop out the cores, and place the pear halves core-side down into the coconut milk to simmer for 15 minutes.

3 Once the wine has reduced by half, remove the cinnamon stick and lower the heat to medium. Continue simmering until it becomes a thick syrup, then remove from the heat.

4 Turn the pears over and slowly simmer on the other side for 10 minutes. Remove them from the poaching liquid. Place one pear half into a shallow dish and spoon over some of the coconut poaching liquid. Drizzle with the wine sauce and garnish with a sprig of mint.

Fig and Lavender Honey Yogurt Pie

Serves 10 to 12

Summertime begs for cool, no-bake desserts, and this is one of the best, with no mixer or special equipment required.

- 1⅓ cups graham cracker crumbs
- 5 tablespoons unsalted butter, melted
- ½ cup quick cooking oats
- 3 tablespoons light brown sugar
- 1 pinch sea salt
- 1 tablespoon unflavored gelatin
- 3 tablespoons cold water
- 1 cup Greek-style yogurt
- ½ cup lavender honey
- 1½ cups heavy cream, chilled
- 12 purple mission figs, quartered lengthwise

1 Stir together the graham cracker crumbs, melted butter, oats, brown sugar, and salt until moistened. Press into the bottom of a 6-inch springform pan and halfway up the sides, packing it tightly with your fingertips so it is even and compacted.

2 Sprinkle the gelatin over the cold water in a small sauté pan and let soften for

Did You Know This Crap?

Greek-style yogurt is used in this recipe with fantastic results. It has a thicker, creamier consistency than regular yogurt because it has been strained to remove the excess liquid. You can also change up the recipe by topping this dessert with the Plum Champagne Granita (p. 236) instead of the figs.

Crappy Little Kitchens

2 minutes. Whisk together the yogurt and honey in a medium-size bowl. Set the small sauté pan over the lowest flame possible while stirring constantly, just until it melts. Whisk the melted gelatin into the yogurt mixture until smooth.

3 Whip the heavy cream until it holds stiff peaks. Gently fold half of the whipped cream into the yogurt mixture, taking care not to deflate the cream. Now fold the last of the whipped cream into the yogurt mixture. Gently spoon the mixture into the prepared springform pan, then cover the pan with plastic wrap, and refrigerate it until completely set, at least 6 hours and up to 1 day.

4 Hold a small knife under hot tap water, and then run it along the sides of the pie to help release it from the pan. Open the spring, and slice the pie into wedges. Serve each slice on a dessert plate. Place 2 pieces of fig on top of each slice, and scatter a few fig pieces on the plate. Serve ice cold.

Phil's Fourth of July Birthday Cobbler

Serves 8 to 10

This festive red, white, and blue dessert can be easily mixed by hand in any CLK.

12 ounces unsalted butter

1 cup half-and-half

3 cups all-purpose flour

2 teaspoons baking powder

2 cups sugar

2 tablespoons sea salt

2 eggs

3 tablespoons tapioca flour or cornstarch

1 teaspoon cinnamon

1 pinch nutmeg

3 pints fresh blueberries

2 pounds fresh strawberries, prepped and quartered

Vanilla ice cream, as needed

1 Preheat your oven to 350°. Melt 8 ounces of the butter in the microwave (on full power for about 1 minute), then add the half-and-half to cool it down. Set it aside.

2 In a medium bowl, whisk together the flour, baking powder, ½ cup of sugar, and 1 tablespoon of salt. In the center of these dry ingredients, crack the 2 eggs and lightly scramble them. Add the butter and half-and-half mixture into the eggs, and stir until the dough just comes together. Refrigerate.

3 In a large bowl, whisk together 1½ cup of sugar, 1 tablespoon of salt, tapioca, cinnamon, and nutmeg. Melt 4 ounces of butter and add it to the sugar mixture. Toss in the berries and completely coat them with sugar and butter. Evenly spread this on the bottom of a 13 x 9-inch baking pan.

4 Drop large dumplings of your refrigerated dough onto the pan of berries. Each dumpling should represent one portion of cobbler, so try to make them even and barely touching. Bake this in the oven for 45 minutes or until golden brown, and then let it rest 10 minutes.

5 Scoop each cobbler helping into an individual serving bowl and top with a generous scoop of vanilla ice cream.

Chocolate Rum Cheesecake with Vanilla Espresso Syrup

Serves 10 to 12

If a fabulous cheesecake and a brilliant cup of coffee had a love child, this would be their gourmet story.

1½ cups graham cracker crumbs

6 tablespoons unsalted butter, melted

½ cup quick cooking oats

3 tablespoons light brown sugar

2 pinches sea salt

6 ounces semisweet chocolate

⅓ cup dark rum

1 pound cream cheese, softened

5 ounces ricotta cheese

1¾ cups sugar

2 tablespoons cocoa powder

1 teaspoon pure vanilla extract

2 eggs

1 cup freshly brewed espresso or very strong coffee

1 vanilla bean, scraped

1 Preheat the oven to 350°. Line the bottom of an 8-inch springform pan with parchment paper. Mix the graham cracker crumbs, melted butter, oats, brown sugar, and a pinch of salt until moistened. Press into the bottom of your lined pan, packing it tightly with your fingertips.

2 In a microwave-safe bowl, microwave the chocolate and rum in short intervals until completely melted and smooth when stirred. In a large bowl, combine the cream cheese, ricotta, 1 cup sugar, cocoa, pinch of salt, and vanilla extract until smooth. Then whisk in 1 egg at a time. Slowly add the melted chocolate and rum mixture until just combined. Pour the cheesecake mixture into the springform pan and place in the oven.

3 Bake 45 minutes or until set in the middle. As soon as you take it out of the oven, run a knife around the outside of the cheesecake to release it, and place in the refrigerator to chill.

4 Put your 1-quart saucepot over medium-high heat and stir the espresso, ¾ cup of sugar, and vanilla bean until the sugar is dissolved. Allow it to simmer for 10 minutes or until it thickens slightly. Strain out the vanilla bean by pouring the sauce through your fine strainer and refrigerate. Cut the chilled cheesecake into slices and serve drizzled with the sauce.

Berry Short Cakes with Vanilla Bean Mousse

These cakes are actually little cream biscuits because I fold in cream, which is a much easier task for the CLK chef than cutting in cold butter. For a restaurant-worthy presentation, finish this off with a drizzle of chocolate sauce and a sprig of mint.

2 cups all-purpose flour, plus more for dusting

¼ cup sugar, plus more for dusting

2 teaspoons baking powder

1 teaspoon sea salt

3 cups heavy cream

1 vanilla bean, scraped

3 tablespoons powdered sugar

8 ounces cream cheese, softened

1 teaspoon pure vanilla extract

3 pounds fresh berries

1 Preheat the oven to 400°. In a medium bowl, sift together the flour, sugar, baking powder, and sea salt. Pour in the 1½ cups of heavy cream, and mix until it comes together into a ball of dough. If it is a little too dry to adhere together, add more cream a tablespoon at a time until it is soft but not sticky.

2 Lightly flour your clean and dry counter. Placing the dough on the counter, fold it over to knead it twice, and shape it into a perfect square. Roll out your square (with a rolling pin if you have one, but I use a wine bottle in my CLK) until it is ½-inch thick. Cut the dough into 2-inch squares and then diagonally to make triangles. Place them on a sheet tray, dust them with sugar, and bake for 10 to 15 minutes or until golden brown. Always eat a fresh biscuit to check for doneness, and because it would be silly not to!

3 Place 1½ cups heavy cream into a large bowl and add the vanilla bean seeds. Whisk slowly to try to break the seeds apart while adding the powdered sugar. Now whip the cream to stiff peaks and refrigerate.

4 In another large bowl, stir together the softened cream cheese and the vanilla extract. Add half of the whipped cream and fold it together by gently putting your spatula in the center of the bowl and pulling it towards you while you scrape the spatula along the bottom. When the spatula breaks the surface of the batter, turn the bowl about an inch, and start again. Each time you pull up and then drop the spatula back into the center, you will be folding in the whipped cream to the batter. Only do this for about 90 seconds or you will deflate all of your fluffy cream.

5 Place one warm biscuit in the center of the plate. Gently top with a large scoop of mousse, and pile on the berries. Lean another biscuit up against the berries, and top with a small dollop of mousse and a vibrant berry. Serve immediately.

Plum Champagne Granita

Oh-so-very-sophisticated served in a frozen martini or wine glass, this recipe is also foolproof. You can make it well in advance because it will remain spectacular in your freezer for 2 weeks. Also a beautiful garnish on other desserts, I use it to top the Fig and Lavender Honey Yogurt Pie (p. 230).

1 pound red plums,
   pitted, chopped

¼ cup sugar

¼ cup water

⅔ cup champagne

1 Place the plums, sugar, and water in a blender and puree until smooth. Pour into a baking dish large enough to accommodate all the puree plus room for adding the champagne. Stir the champagne into the plum puree. Freeze until the puree is icy around the edges, about 1 hour. Using a large fork, stir the icy parts of the puree into the middle of the dish. Continue to freeze for about 2½ hours or until the mixture is frozen, stirring the edges into the center every 30 minutes.

2 Using the fork, scrape the granita into flaky crystals. Wrap the dish tightly with plastic wrap and place in the freezer along with six wine glasses. Allow the glasses to chill for about an hour or until they have a lovely frost on them. Fill them with the granita, and serve like a fine wine.

Prairie Pound Cake

Serves 10 to 12

A kaleidoscope of flavors, this cake will be a gourmet experience for everyone. Make certain that the butter is at room temperature so the cake whips right up when you mix it by hand.

2 cups fine yellow cornmeal

1 cup all-purpose flour

1 teaspoon sea salt

1 teaspoon ground cinnamon

8 ounces unsalted butter, room temperature, plus more for pan

2 cups sugar

7 eggs

¼ cup whiskey

¼ cup clover honey

1 Preheat the oven to 350°. Whisk the cornmeal, flour, salt, and cinnamon together in a medium-size bowl and set it aside.

2 In a large bowl, whisk the butter and sugar together until light and fluffy. Add the eggs one at a time, beating well after each addition. Fold in the cornmeal mixture until just blended.

3 Grease a bundt cake pan or disposable tube pan with butter or cooking spray, and pour in the cake batter. Bake for 50 minutes, or until the cake is golden brown and a toothpick comes out clean.

4 While the cake is baking, add the whiskey to your 1-quart saucepot and place it over high heat. When it comes to a boil, reduce the heat to medium and stir in the honey. Simmer for 5 minutes, remove from the heat, and chill.

5 When the cake is finished baking, allow it to cool for 10 minutes before inverting it onto your serving platter. Brush on the whiskey honey glaze (yes, use all of it!), cover the cake with tin foil or plastic wrap, and store it on the counter overnight. This cake is best served the second day because the brushed on glaze has time to sink in and infuse the cake with flavor.

Citrus Peach Upside-Down Cake

Serves 10 to 12 A stunningly beautiful cake, bake it just once to see what I mean. If you can't find orange blossom honey, substitute any honey you think tastes wonderful or you already have in your crappy little pantry.

3 fresh peaches, halved and pitted (about 1 pound)

2 lemons, zested and juiced

3 limes, zested and juiced

2 tablespoons plus ½ cup orange blossom honey

6 ounces plus 1 tablespoon unsalted butter, room temperature

¾ cup all-purpose flour

1 teaspoon baking powder

1 pinch sea salt

¾ cup sugar

4 eggs

Powdered sugar, as needed

Whipped cream, as needed

1 Preheat the oven to 350°. Slice each peach half into four wedges. Place them in your 1-quart stockpot and stir in the lemon juice, lime juice, 2 tablespoons of honey, and 1 tablespoon of butter. Heat this over medium heat for 5 minutes or until the peaches soften slightly and the juices thicken. Set this aside to cool.

2 Line the bottom of a round 8-inch cake pan with parchment paper. Whisk the flour, baking powder, and salt in a medium bowl and set aside. Using your whisk, beat the 6 ounces of butter, sugar, 2 tablespoons of lemon zest, and 1 tablespoon of lime zest in a large bowl until light and fluffy. The butter must be at room temperature to whip up easily. Add the eggs one at a time, beating well after each addition before adding the next. Fold in the flour mixture by gently putting your spatula in the center of the bowl and pulling it toward you while scraping the spatula along the bottom. When the spatula breaks the surface of the batter, turn the bowl about an inch, and start again. Each time you pull up and then drop the spatula back into the center, you will fold the flour into the batter. Only do this for about 90 seconds or you will overmix the batter and your cake could turn out tough.

3 Pour the ½ cup of honey evenly over the bottom of the lined cake pan. Arrange the peaches in a single layer over the honey. I usually do mine to resemble a fan that goes in a circle, but make whatever pattern you find attractive. Carefully spoon the cake batter over the peaches, and spread it out evenly, while disturbing the peaches as little as possible.

4 Bake for 15 minutes. Then rotate the cake, reduce the heat to 300°, and continue baking for 1 hour or until the cake is golden brown on top and begins to pull away from the sides of the pan.

5 Don't allow the cake to cool for more than 5 minutes or it will not easily release from the pan. Run a knife around the sides of the pan to loosen the cake. Place a cake platter upside down over the cake pan. Using a towel to hold the hot cake pan, turn it upside down onto the platter.

6 Cut the cake into wedges and serve warm, dusted with powdered sugar and a dollop of whipped cream.

My Better Half Groom's Cake

Serves 8 to 10

Look for organic applesauce and match the apple to the variety used in the sauce. For example, if you find organic applesauce made with gala apples, use gala apple slices. You can "sift" the dry ingredients by sending them through your fine strainer or by whisking them together.

2¾ cups all-purpose flour

1 teaspoon baking soda

1 teaspoon baking powder

1½ teaspoons cinnamon

½ teaspoon nutmeg

½ teaspoon sea salt

1 cup unsalted butter, room temperature, plus more for pans

2 cups sugar

2 eggs

2½ cups organic applesauce

1 teaspoon pure vanilla extract

1 cup chopped pecans, toasted

1 apple, quartered and thinly sliced

2 tablespoons Calvados (apple brandy)

Powdered sugar, as needed

1 Preheat the oven to 350°. In a medium bowl sift together the flour, baking soda, baking powder, cinnamon, nutmeg, and salt. Set aside.

2 Use your whisk to whip the room temperature butter and half of the sugar until it is light and fluffy. Add the rest of the sugar and then the eggs one at a time, beating well after each addition. Mix in the applesauce and vanilla before folding in the flour and the pecans.

3 Butter two 8-inch round cake pans, and divide the cake batter between the 2 pans. Bake for 25 to 30 minutes or until brown and a toothpick comes out clean.

4 While the cake bakes, place the sliced apple and the Calvados into your 8-inch sauté pan over medium heat. Gently stir until the apples are soft and have absorbed the brandy.

5 When finished baking, allow the cake to cool for 10 minutes before inverting one pan onto your serving platter. Layer the apple slices on top of this cake round, and then invert the second round onto the layer of apple. Dust the entire cake with powdered sugar by dropping a tablespoon or so into your fine strainer and shaking it over the cake.

Individual Sour Cherry Tiramisus

Normally making a tiramisu from scratch takes several hours, mainly because of all the time needed for the custard between the cookies to set up. With this version, I make a mousse instead of custard so there's no set-up time needed, and I love the deconstructed presentation.

1 pound cherries, pitted and halved

1 cup vodka

¼ cup freshly squeezed lemon juice

6 tablespoons sugar

8 ounces mascarpone cheese, softened

1 cup heavy cream

2 tablespoons powdered sugar

½ cup freshly brewed espresso (or very strong coffee)

16 lady fingers, Italian sponge biscuits

Your favorite bar of chocolate shaved with vegetable peeler

1 In your 12-inch sauté pan, combine the cherries, vodka, lemon juice, and 3 tablespoons of sugar, stirring until the sugar has dissolved. Allow the cherries to soak for 20 minutes, and then place the pot over medium heat. When it comes to a simmer, use a slotted spoon to scoop the cherries into a medium bowl. Continue reducing the cherry sauce for about 15 minutes until it reaches a thick syrup, and then remove it from the heat.

2 Fold the mascarpone into the bowl of cherries, and set aside. In a large bowl, whip the heavy cream and powdered sugar to stiff peaks. Fold half of the whipped cream into the cherry mascarpone, then fold in the rest, and set it in the refrigerator.

3 In a small bowl, stir 3 tablespoons of sugar into the espresso until it dissolves. Quickly dip each lady finger into the sweet espresso and set two alongside each other on a dessert plate. Scoop a large dollop of cherry mousse on top, then place two more cookies turned in the opposite direction on the mousse. Top with a small spoon of mousse. Drizzle the vodka cherry syrup around the dessert, and sprinkle with the chocolate shavings.

Grasshopper Layer Cake

Serves 10 to 12

Butter is what makes a cake tender. This recipe combines the butter with milk, making the cake tender yet able to hold its shape. By melting the butter, this cake batter stirs together in minutes with no elbow grease at all!

2 cups all-purpose flour

1½ cups sugar, plus more for pans

½ cup unsweetened cocoa

1¼ teaspoons baking powder

1 teaspoon baking soda

1 teaspoon sea salt

8 ounces unsalted butter, plus 2 tablespoons more for topping

1 cup whole milk

3 eggs

1 tablespoon pure vanilla extract

2 cups heavy cream

2 teaspoons pure mint extract

2 tablespoons powdered sugar

8 ounces dark chocolate (60 to 70% cocoa)

2 tablespoons light corn syrup

1 Preheat the oven to 350°. Sift the flour, sugar, cocoa, baking powder, baking soda, and salt into a large bowl. Make a well in the middle of these dry ingredients, and add the 8 ounces of melted butter, milk, eggs, and vanilla extract. Mix this all together until it is smooth. Butter two 8-inch round cake pans and then lightly dust with sugar, and divide the cake batter between the 2 pans. Bake for 30 minutes or until a toothpick comes out clean. Allow them to cool for 10 minutes, and turn the cakes out onto cooling racks. Cool for another 20 minutes.

2 While the cakes are cooling, use your whisk to whip the heavy cream, 1½ teaspoons of mint extract, and powdered sugar to stiff peaks. Place in the refrigerator.

3 In a microwave-safe bowl, combine the dark chocolate, 2 tablespoons of butter, corn syrup, and remaining ½ teaspoon of mint extract. Microwave for 30 seconds, and then stir. Microwave in 10-second intervals until the chocolate sauce is uniformly melted and smooth.

4 When the cake is completely cool, use a long strand of dental floss (mint is fine in this case!) to cut horizontally through the center of each cake round. Then cut horizontally through each piece again making 4 thin cake disks. Place one disk in the center of your cake platter, and top it evenly with ⅓ of the mint whipped cream. Top with another cake disk, ⅓ of the whipped cream, a cake disk, the final ⅓ of whipped cream, and then the final cake disk. Spread the chocolate sauce over the cake, allowing some to drizzle down the sides. Cut into wedges and be prepared to be amazed at what you've created. To present, I do little more than to stand a beautifully layered slice on a plate.

Sweet Cheese Cranberry Purses

Serves 12

The humble cheese Danish inspired this recipe. I changed the design to resemble a trendy purse and incorporated a vibrant melt-in-your-mouth center.

2 cups fresh cranberries

1 tablespoon lemon zest

2 tablespoons orange zest

¼ cup orange juice

1 teaspoon pure vanilla extract

3 tablespoons sugar, plus more for dusting

15 ounces cream cheese, room temperature

½ cup honey

2 sheets (one box) frozen puff pastry thawed

¼ cup heavy cream

1 Preheat the oven to 350°. In your 1-quart saucepot, combine your cranberries, lemon zest, orange zest, orange juice, vanilla extract, and sugar and place them over medium heat. Cook slowly until the cranberries soften, remove from the heat, and refrigerate.

2 In a small bowl, stir the cream cheese and honey together until smooth. Cut the puff pastry into 3-inch squares. You should get six per sheet. Place the puff pastry squares on your work space and drop a tablespoon of honey cream cheese into the center of each. Now drop a tablespoon of cranberry mixture onto each. Pull up the corners and pinch them together

Swap It

Instead of tart cranberries, feel free to use blueberries, raspberries, or cherries for the filling.

tightly (so they don't pop open) to create little purses.

3 Place the purses 1 inch apart on a baking sheet, brush them with cream, and dust with sugar. Bake for 15 to 20 minutes until golden brown and crispy on the outside. Allow the purses to cool for 8 minutes before serving.

Heavenly Cheesecake

Serves 8 to 10

Most cheesecakes, even good ones, tend to be incredibly dense and heavy. My cheesecake eats like a heavenly cloud because I use mascarpone cheese, which is softer and lighter than commonly used cream cheese.

1½ cups graham cracker crumbs

6 tablespoons unsalted butter, melted

½ cup quick cooking oats

3 tablespoons light brown sugar

2 pinches sea salt

15 ounces Ricotta cheese

1 pound Mascarpone cheese, room temperature

1 cup sugar

2 teaspoons pure vanilla extract

4 eggs

3 egg yolks

1 Preheat the oven to 350° and line an 8-inch springform pan with parchment paper. Stir together the graham cracker crumbs, melted butter, oats, brown sugar, and salt until moistened. Press into the bottom of the springform pan, packing it tightly with your fingertips so it is even and compacted.

2 In a large bowl combine the ricotta, mascarpone, sugar, pinch of salt, and vanilla extract. Stir until smooth, and then whip in 1 egg and then 1 egg yolk at a time. Pour the cheesecake mixture into the springform pan and place in the oven.

Swap It

If you like, you can substitute cream cheese plus two tablespoons of honey for the mascarpone cheese in this recipe.

3 Bake for 50 minutes or until golden brown and set in the middle. As soon as you take it out of the oven, run a knife around the outside of the cheesecake to release it from the side of the pan and set the whole thing in the refrigerator until chilled. Cut into slices. The light decadence of this dessert lends itself well to kiwi, passion fruit, strawberries, grapes, or chocolate. Arrange the fruit in a fanlike pattern over the entire cheesecake for a beautiful table presentation, or over a single slice for individual servings.

Mexican Chocolate Soup

Serves 6 to 8 This recipe began as a warm chocolate pudding with a bit of a kick, but by thinning the pudding I created a lighter version that is ever-so-pleasing to the palate.

2 cups whole milk

2 tablespoons sugar

2 Ancho chilies, dried

5 ounces semisweet chocolate, chopped

5 ounces dark chocolate, chopped

2 cups heavy cream

2 cups whipped cream, unsweetened

Red chili powder, for garnish

1 In your 1-quart saucepot, place the milk, sugar, and Ancho chilies over medium heat. Stir to dissolve the sugar and soften the chili, and bring to a simmer for 10 to 15 minutes.

2 Place the chocolates in a large bowl, and pour the hot milk mixture over the chocolate. Whisk the milk and chocolate together until the chocolate melts.

3 Add the heavy cream to a heavy-bottom stockpot, and place it over medium heat. When it begins to simmer, slowly whisk in the chocolate mixture, and continue whisking until everything is combined and smooth. Turn the heat down to low, and allow the chili to steep for 8 minutes.

4 Place a fine strainer over another large pot, and carefully strain the chocolate soup to remove any chili stem and seeds. Replace over the lowest heat until you are ready to serve. Ladle soup into each serving bowl or coffee cup, top with a dollop of whipped cream, and dust lightly with chili powder. Serve immediately or the cream will melt.

Swap It

If you want to tone down the spice, use only one chili. For the kid at heart in all of us, feel free to use marshmallow "croutons" instead of whipped cream to top this souper dessert.

Mike Modano's Favorite Cookies

Yield
15 to 20
Cookies

This recipe is very CLK friendly because you don't need a mixer to cream the butter and sugar, just a little elbow grease. Thank you Chef Jeffery Hobbs for introducing me to the ultimate chocolate chip cookie that you've served to Mike Modano of the Dallas Stars.

6 ounces unsalted butter, melted

1 cup packed light brown sugar

½ cup sugar

1 whole egg plus one yolk

2 teaspoons pure vanilla extract

2 cups plus 2 tablespoons all-purpose flour

½ teaspoon sea salt

½ teaspoon baking soda

2 cups bittersweet chocolate chips (60% cocoa or substitute semi sweet)

1 cup pecan pieces, toasted

1 Preheat oven to 325°. Melt the butter in the microwave but allow it to cool down a bit to keep from melting the chocolate prematurely. Using your whisk, combine the butter and sugar together in a large bowl. Whisk in the egg, egg yolk, and vanilla.

2 In a medium bowl, sift together the flour, sea salt and baking soda. Add this flour mixture to the butter and egg mixture and fold until just combined. Fold in the chocolate and pecan pieces. Be careful not to overmix.

3 Take a ¼ cup measure, and portion out your cookie dough onto a sheet tray, placing each cookie about 3 inches apart. Bake the cookies for 15 to 20 minutes, turning the sheet tray around once to bake them evenly. Take them out when they are just golden brown around the edges. Allow the cookies to cool on the tray and store whatever cookies are left (they'll go fast!) in an airtight container.

Brandy Chocolate Truffles

Yields about 24

Indulge your friends with homemade truffles as a holiday gift. I like to roll mine in a combination of hazelnuts, pecans, and pistachios for a festive multicolored coating.

1 cup heavy cream

12 ounces bittersweet chocolate, chopped

2 ounces brandy

1 cup assorted finely ground nuts

1 In your 1-quart saucepot, place the heavy cream over medium heat. While waiting for it to come to a simmer, stir the chocolate and brandy together in a medium bowl.

2 Once the cream begins to bubble up in the pot, carefully pour it into the bowl of chocolate. Whisk together until smooth, and then pour into a one-quart baking dish. Wrap it tightly and refrigerate until completely solid, which should take an hour.

3 Place the nuts into a shallow bowl. Scoop out 1 tablespoon of truffle mix, and form it into a ball. Then roll it in the nuts until well coated. Roll it between your palms to make it as round as possible. Roll it one last time through the nuts. Repeat until all the truffle mix is gone. Store in an airtight container in the refrigerator until ready to serve. For a romantic single serving presentation, serve the truffles in a small gift box for each guest to be opened at the table. For a platter presentation, stack them neatly in a pyramid.

How to "Fine Grind" Nuts with No Grinder

You don't need a special grinder to create finely ground nuts. Just put the nuts in a freezer bag and place your sauce pot on top. Put pressure on the sauce pot, rocking it back and forth to crush the nuts until you reach a fine consistency. Most grocery stores sell bags of ground nuts in their baking section as well, if you'd prefer to buy a finished product.

Dad's Miraculous Pineapple Upside-Down Campfire Cake

Serves
10 to 12

Here's the recipe for my dad's amazing pineapple upside-down cake that you can make from the confines of your cozy CLK. No campfire needed!

⅔ cup firmly packed light brown sugar

2 ounces unsalted butter, melted

3 cups fresh pineapple chunks, about 1 pineapple

¾ cup all-purpose flour

1 teaspoon baking powder

1 pinch sea salt

6 ounces unsalted butter, room temperature

¾ cup sugar

4 eggs

1 Preheat the oven to 350°. Line the bottom of a round 8-inch cake pan with parchment paper and spray with cooking spray. In a small bowl, stir together the brown sugar and melted butter, and spread it evenly in the bottom of the pan. Arrange the pineapple chunks on top of the sugar tightly packing them in, but only a single layer.

2 Whisk the flour, baking powder, and salt in a medium bowl and set aside. Then use your whisk to beat the butter and sugar in a large bowl until light and fluffy. The butter must be at room temperature to whip up easily. Add the eggs one at a time, beating well after each addition before adding the next.

3 Fold in the flour mixture by gently putting your spatula in the center of the bowl. Pull toward you and scrape the spatula along the bottom. When the spatula breaks the surface of the batter, turn the bowl about an inch, and start again. Each time you pull up and then drop the spatula back into the center, you will be folding in the flour to the batter. Only do this for about 90 seconds, or you will overmix the cake.

4 Carefully spoon the cake batter over the pineapple, and spread it out evenly, while disturbing the pineapple as little as possible.

Crappy Little Kitchens

5 Bake for 15 minutes. Then rotate the cake, reduce the heat to 300°, and continue baking for 1 hour or until the cake is golden brown on top and beginning to pull away from the sides of the pan.

6 Don't allow the cake to cool for more than 5 minutes or it will not easily release from the pan. Run a knife around the sides of the pan to loosen the cake. Place a cake platter upside down over the cake pan. Using a towel to hold the hot cake pan, turn it upside down onto the platter. It's ready to eat!

Acknowledgments

Gourmet Meals in Crappy Little Kitchens was written and created by me, but the inspiration and content of this book was born of many wonderful relationships. Here I would like to acknowledge as many of the spectacular people who have influenced me as possible.

My mom and dad probably wouldn't call themselves chefs, but the important thing they gave me was that food should be a celebration. The whole family would come together to make giant pans of lasagna, and my father would light up. Every opportunity we have to gather begets a massive outdoor cookout to rival anything seen on cable. Each of my parents makes what they make very well. My mother can do things with tuna and macaroni and cheese that just curls my toes. My dad still makes the best pork ribs I've ever tasted, and that's not just because I love them. It's because they are wonderful.

My sisters would be interested in cooking even if I wasn't, but I am, so they ARE my band wagon. As a family we travel to cook offs, all wearing Crappy Little Kitchen T-shirts and passing out CLK propaganda. My little sisters and I (yes I'm the oldest) try restaurants together, travel and plan where we'll be eating long before the plane and hotel arrangements are set, and talk about food endlessly. Truly, we don't choose our family, but I would pick my sisters to be my best friends even if they were people I'd met late in my life. The fact that we've known each other literally forever only makes our relationship better.

My grandmothers each do something amazingly well. Granny Dee can stretch eggs and cheese for days with her signature dish, creamed eggs on toast. My mother was usually the one who made "cup of egg" (soft boiled egg cracked over toast that I got to tear into little pieces in a coffee cup) for me, but Dee taught her. Both dishes bring tears to my eyes. Granny Ila makes the best homemade candy you've ever tried whether you know it or not. Pink divinity and chocolate fudge at Christmas are a must. It's magical to see her go outside and say, "No, it's too humid today. We'll see if we can make candy tomorrow." Watching her drop the boiled sugar into a bowl of water and roll it around in her fingers to see if it's reached the hard ball stage . . . has affected me and made me need to learn more.

Jay, ever my friend and partner, our relationship has changed much over the past 12 years I've known him, but our camaraderie in the kitchen stays the same. His signature dish would be his "bachelor chow," but it changes every time he makes it, so the recipe will be difficult to nail down.

My friends are amazing. Amy insists that she can't cook, but still makes the best chicken pot pie I've ever tasted (sorry Jeffery you're coming up). She inspires me in so many aspects of my life, whenever I'm trying to look or act like an adult I always look to her and her stellar example of a woman. Laura always has an immaculate kitchen, and she goes on wonderful culinary adventures with me to restaurants and wineries. She makes the BEST chocolate pie in the world! My little Pound Cake, my best friend, Sarah Lee, makes all sorts of tasty things from cucumber kimchi to scallion pancakes, but her friendship is what gives my life flavor. Woolley's the greatest flatmate ever, and not just because of his mother's legendary refried beans.

The chefs who I've worked with truly make me humble. Jon and Joe were my first bosses when I was a lowly dishwasher. They taught me how to have fun despite the long, hot, grueling hours. I'm very proud of the menus we put out at Savory, and I am so fond of the memories of the prep meetings that would end (if we were lucky, sometimes we had to go back to work) with burgers at The Landing at 2:00 AM. Any restaurant I run will have a menu patterned after Savory.

Gilbert and Jeffery probably influenced this book the most. When I put it down for a while, and then picked it up for the final edit it truly hit me how much these men helped me. Gilbert definitely has the best pallet of any chef I've worked with, he could taste my pesto and tell me what day I made it. Jeffery not only taught me nearly everything I know about demi, salt and pepper, and cookies, he's been an inspiration in life and I'm so glad he's my friend.

Brian and Karin are some of my favorite people in the whole world. I gotta say it, the Grape was the most awful, debilitating work schedule I've ever encountered. Often fourteen-hour days and sometimes seven days a week. Gotta tell you, it was one of my favorite work experiences because of the environment those two created. The crew always got breakfast, lunch, and dinner. We had fun, we loved each other. Chuy, Rosa, Bobby, and Juanita, I love you and I miss you!!

Lenny and Jason came along at a time when I really needed allies in the work place. Lenny is a master at fresh Asian cooking, he is after all a true California boy at heart, but I'll always remember him for the Apple Dapple! Not just any war hero, if I'm worthy, Lenny and I will be friends forever. Jason is the quintessential French man, but we have a lot of fun thinking outside the box. Egg yolk ravioli with bacon pesto or even butter-infused poached eggs are a few of the many recipes we have rolling around in our heads.

The people who have helped directly with the book, I can't thank you enough. Rosemary my agent has been a godsend. None of this would have happened without her, and I just love her accent so much I could die. I never knew what agents really did until we started looking and negotiating with publishers, and let me tell the other would-be authors out there . . . get yourself a literary agent! HCI publishing, especially Michele, thank you so much for your time and kindness with this first-time author. You're the best!

index